# Critical Thinking Secrets

*Discover the Practical Fundamental Skills and Tools That Are Essential to Improve Your Critical Thinking, Problem Solving, and Decision Making Skills*

# Table of Contents

Chapter 1: Introduction ..................................................................................................... 4

Chapter 2: What is Critical Thinking and Why is it Important? ................................... 6

    Summary of The Conceptualization of Critical Thinking ......................................... 7

    10 Traits of Critical Thinkers ........................................................................................ 8

    Benefits of Critical Thinking ........................................................................................ 10

Chapter 3: Skills You Will Develop ..................................................................................... 12

    Crucial Critical Thinking Skills .................................................................................... 12

Chapter 4: Why Critical Thinking? ..................................................................................... 17

    Critical Thinking at the Workplace ............................................................................. 19

    Critical Thinking in College .......................................................................................... 21

    Critical Thinking in the Real World ............................................................................ 22

Chapter 5: Practical Ways to Improve Critical Thinking ................................................. 23

    Critical Thinking Exercise ............................................................................................. 23

    Don't Waste Time ........................................................................................................... 23

    Learn Something New Every Day ................................................................................ 24

    No Boundaries for Learning ......................................................................................... 24

    Always Question ............................................................................................................. 25

    Active Listening .............................................................................................................. 26

    Solve Just the Problem .................................................................................................. 28

    Improving Critical Thinking Every Day ..................................................................... 29

    How to Sharpen Your Logical Thinking Skills .......................................................... 30

    7 Ways to Think More Critically ................................................................................... 33

    Ways to Improve Our Critical Thinking ..................................................................... 35

Chapter 6: How to Implement Critical Thinking .............................................................. 37

    Developing Critical Thinking ........................................................................................ 55

    5 Steps to Asking Good Questions .................................................................. 57

# Chapter 7: Common Critical Thinking Pitfalls and How to Avoid Them ................ 61

    Three Basic Building Blocks of Critical Thinking ............................................... 61

    Vagueness ........................................................................................................... 67

    Ambiguity .......................................................................................................... 68

    The Claim and its Sources ................................................................................. 69

    Fallacy ................................................................................................................ 70

    Rhetoric ............................................................................................................. 76

# Chapter 8: How Critical Thinking Affects Your Life .............................................. 94

# Chapter 9: Conclusion ............................................................................................ 96

# Chapter 1: Introduction

Critical thinking is the ability to analyze facts and information to make rational decisions, and understand the logical connection between ideas. It also involves the ability to engage in reflective and independent thinking. Critical thinking is a complex subject and there are a lot of definitions given to it. In general, it is the ability to evaluate factual evidence to make decisions rationally by making use of the information available.

Critical thinking is more about using available information based on experience and facts to solve problems and knowing where to find it. A person who has a good memory and knows many things does not imply that he or she can think critically. Gathering information is one thing, using it effectively is another.

Though its name seems to suggest otherwise, critical thinking does not imply being argumentative or critical of others. It can be used in avoiding fallacies, bad reasoning, and it can also play a very significant role in cooperative reasoning and constructive tasks. It can make our arguments more compelling, in addition to helping us gather facts and knowledge. Moreover, critical thinking can also be used to improve our work processes and enhance social institutions.

Those with good critical thinking skills can:
- Reflect on the justification of one's own beliefs and values
- Recognize the relevance and necessity of ideas
- Fix problems systematically
- Identify inconsistencies and common reasoning mistakes
- Recognize, create, and assess arguments
- Understand the logical connections between ideas

Of course, we are not gifted with the ability to make good decisions and reach appropriate conclusions all the time.

The primary tool that we use in making better judgments is critical thinking. Basically, critical thinking is the careful application of reasoning in determining whether or not a claim is true.

Developing the willingness and the ability to apply the critical thinking skills found in this book will make you smarter and help you improve your critical thinking skills with actual practical advice and strategies. The things and lessons that you are going to learn from this book can be applicable to the everyday decisions that you make in your life.

# Chapter 2: What is Critical Thinking and Why is it Important?

There are many different definitions for critical thinking, and generally, all of them emphasize the importance of clarity and rationality in the way we think. Critical thinking is the process of using reasoning to find out what is true and what is false. It plays a very important role in our daily lives because we all make decisions every day, both small and big. After getting up from bed in the morning, we all have to make the decision on what to eat for breakfast, what to wear for the day and more. These are very simple and common decisions that we constantly make. Moreover, we also make decisions that can really have an impact on our lives. These life-changing decisions include, for example, selecting a university in which to pursue higher education or choosing the person to love and marry, etc.

Critical thinkers approach any circumstance in a way that ensures every possible solution is within their control or is something they know of. To put it simply, critical thinking is the process of applying what you know to reach the best possible solution.

Critical thinking is a way of thinking about particular things at a particular time, and it is not about gathering facts and knowledge or something that you can learn once and use it forever.

When we think critically, we can analyze information without bias or prejudice and make decisions accordingly. It also involves the assessment and evaluation of sources such as data, facts, and other phenomena. When we can think critically, we will be able to draw reasonable conclusions from the data, facts, or information and evaluate the information to arrive at the best possible solution to fix a problem or make a decision.

The idea of critical thinking has been the centerpiece of most research in the last 50 years. The words themselves are derived from Greek. "Critical" comes from "kriticos," which means discerning judgment and "kriterion," which means standards. Therefore, the word implies the development of "discerning judgment based on standards."

It is our nature for everyone to think. However, much of our thinking tends to be biased, partial, distorted, and uninformed. The quality of life that we produce depends on the quality of our thoughts. If we think correctly and critically, we can improve the quality of our lives. Badly-constructed thoughts are costly both in money and in quality of life. Better thoughts must be cultivated.

Critical thinking is a mode of thinking about a problem, content, or subject where the thinker wants to improve their thinking skill by skillfully analyzing, evaluating, and reconstructing it.

People who possess well-cultivated critical thinking skills are able to:

- Raise important questions and problems
- Formulate the questions and problems clearly and precisely
- Accumulate and evaluate information using an effective interpretation of abstract ideas that lead to well-reasoned conclusions and feasible solutions
- Think freely with the alternative system of thought
- Communicate effectively with others in finding the solutions to complicated problems

## Summary of The Conceptualization of Critical Thinking

Critical thinking is self-guided thinking that attempts to give a reason at the highest level of quality in an equitable way. People who want to make decisions rationally and reasonably have to think critically and consistently. They are always reminded of the mistakes that human beings make if they do not check carefully before making decisions. They try to decrease the power of their egocentric and sociocentric inclinations and use their own knowledge and what critical thinking offers such as concept and principles to help them improve their thinking skills. These people also know that there are always new things they can learn, no matter how good they are as critical thinkers. There are always other fallacies and mistakes they can make, and irrationalities, prejudices, biases, etc., that they can discover and challenge. They try to improve the world however they can to contribute to a more rational human society.

# 10 Traits of Critical Thinkers

What is a good critical thinker? What are the characteristics of ideal critical thinkers?

1. Spirit of Inquiry

   Effective critical thinkers are broadly interested and generally curious to know more about a wide range of topics. They are more likely to be curious about the world and people. Being able to understand and appreciate the differences in culture, beliefs, and opinions is another good characteristic of great critical thinkers.

2. Empathy

   There is already enough judgment and separation in the world. As we all want to help other people to acquire critical thinking skills, we should not ignore that critical thinking also needs to be emotional and instinctual as much as it is intellectual. That is why critical thinkers need to act with their hearts along with their minds.

3. Be Aware

   We need to be aware that we can stop and think about something critically at any moment. Good critical thinkers are always ready and alert for an opportunity to use their best critical thinking skills in any situation. This enthusiasm to think critically about even the simplest problems and tasks shows the desire for constructive results. Critical thinking also means that we do not accept something easily, but we look and explore all sides of the issue and remain curious to know more about the facts.

4. Be Decisive

   Many situations require you to be quick and decisive, especially those that involve critical thinking. When we apply critical thinking in solving problems, we will weigh our options and expect results at the moment with speed and clarity. Effective critical thinkers are also able to put away their fear when making decisions because they are sure about the decisions they are going making and the results that they are going to get. Critical thinkers do not like to keep things backward, and they always try to move forward and avoid procrastination. Moreover, we have to make decisions even though we still do not have enough information that is needed to make decisions with confidence. When we are faced with such a problem, we become uncertain and let those who are making the final decision make it, although they may not know as much as you do. Effective critical thinkers always understand, more or less, that they will have to make decisions even though they realize that they may end up making the wrong ones. If possible, they would rather not decide at all.

5. Be Honest

   Honesty is important, especially in critical thinking. Effective critical thinking includes things such as moral integrity, ethical consideration, and actions. However, honesty remains at the core of all these things. People with honesty have a strong desire for harmony in the world and to attain this outcome requires honesty in all relationships and collaborations between human beings.

   How we look within ourselves to accept what is there is also the practice of honesty in critical thinking. Critical thinkers also equally see themselves as other people.

6. Have Willingness

   In the following things, we will need the willingness to:
   - We have to learn from our own personal mistakes and faults
   - We have to challenge the situation where needed
   - We have to be open-minded and accept the opinions of other people
   - We also have to think about their opinions and views with the introduction of new evidence
   - We have to be active listeners

   We have to always keep improving, learning, and performing well

7. Be Creative

   It is true that effective critical thinkers are often creative thinkers. Creativity is really essential in business, marketing, and other professional careers. These kinds of jobs relyheavily on creativity. When businesses are able to produce creative products and effective advertisement, their business will be able to run into the global marketplace.

8. Persistence

   Staying focused on the task with great perseverance is something that effective critical thinkers need to do, and they know that it is essential to do so. It is the nature of critical thinkers not to give up easily until the solution to the problem is found and the decision is reached. Here, we can say critical thinkers tend to possess a leadership mindset in the way they think about solving problems. This quality trait is not only useful to have but also encourages others in a team-working environment.

9. Be Objective

    Another trait of critical thinkers is to focus on fairness and inclusion of all sides of opinion and concerns. There is no bias in critical thinking, but only embracing and consideration of possibilities. People with critical thinking skills will not allow themselves to be affected by external influences and internal ones like their emotions or feelings.

10. Reflective Ability

    When we are talking about critical thinking, our focus will not simply stop after making decisions and having the outcome. It will be an important area for improvement and reflection on the learning journey for critical thinkers. We should never ignore our own personal mistakes, but should not live with them. We have to learn from them and move on to the next challenge.

Critical thinking is active, purposeful, mindful, logical, and persistent as opposed to passive, superficial, negligent, illogical, and irresolute.

# Benefits of Critical Thinking

With the help of this book, you too can become a more rational thinker. Benefits of critical thinking include:

- Approach: One of the most important learning developments in critical thinking is awareness. This includes being aware of the different approaches to a problem and objectively assessing whether they are viable. Relying on a standard, uniform problem-solving method sets the baseline for problem-solving so that you can get creative and find other, better approaches to increase your chance of success.
- Save time: With a critical thinking mindset, you can tell from the start which information is irrelevant to whatever you are trying to accomplish. Many people tend to

be overwhelmed with too much information from the get-go, so knowing what is relevant to your task saves you a lot of time. Plus, you know that you make a good decision because you use only the data that matters.

- Appreciation for different views: Critical thinking requires you to think objectively on all the views regarding a scenario. You will develop an appreciation of different views because you learn how to judge cultural norms and understand other factors that can influence decision-making. This is a fundamental element in effective teamwork and leadership.

- Better communication: Because critical thinking requires you to analyze and build up facts to support your claim in any given premise, you can become a more effective communicator. You become more aware of communication cues and are able to adapt to them properly. Moreover, when you know your facts and how they line up, you can proceed to present them in a consistent manner, which is pivotal when you are presenting a proposal or idea.

- Decision making: This is rather obvious, but critical thinking leverages your decision-making abilities to another level. You leave intuition or guesswork behind and go into a more analytical and in-depth basis, which leads to better decisions.

- Reason: Being able to reason is also crucial because all your presentations and ideas will be challenged, so you need to defend them. Here, you will learn how to make inductive and deductive reasoning as well as when to use them. Your decisions will be built on reason and logic rather than on emotion or instinct.

# Chapter 3: Skills You Will Develop

In this chapter, we take a look at some of the most essential critical thinking skills you should and will develop after going through this book. We also discuss some of the things you can do to improve each skill, although you will find a more in-depth guide in a later chapter.

## Crucial Critical Thinking Skills

Many skills fall under the critical thinking umbrella, but we have grouped them into six for your convenience. Focusing on these can help you on your journey to becoming a better critical thinker.

## Identification

You need to identify what you are dealing with first before you proceed to approach the problem. This means identifying the root cause or the factors that may influence the situation as well as the situation itself. After getting a lay of the land, you can then proceed to figure out how to improve the situation.

When presented with a problem or scenario, stop and access the situation thoroughly by asking the following questions:

- Who is doing what?
- What is the reason for this happening?
- What are the results? How can they be changed?

## Research

There is this common knowledge that you should drink eight bottles of water a day or some similar figures. It does not take a veteran critical thinker long to figure out that this fact is ambiguous at best because it does not specify the exact volume of water you should be drinking. Do you know where this figure comes from? Researchers who came up with this result were actually funded by companies that sell water bottles. See the problem?

So, when you need to compare arguments about something, make sure that the research behind those arguments is independent because arguments are intended to be persuasive and certain facts and figures presented in their favor may actually lack context or come from unreliable sources. The best way to approach this problem is verification by finding the source of the information and evaluating whether they are presented objectively. So, how do you improve this field?

First, develop a habit of spotting unforced claims. Does the person making that argument cite where they got their facts and figures from? If you ask them or try to find it yourself, but got no clear answer, then this is already a red flag. Moreover, it is worth noting that not all sources are equally valid. There is a difference between popular and scholarly articles, for example. This is basically the difference between science and "pop science."

Popular articles are intended for the general public and are generally shorter. This means that certain information is glossed over and some are so simplified that some technical details are missing. Again, this is for the general public so the language is simple and easy for general readers to understand and the article may contain photographs, graphics, or visuals to help readers understand. Such articles cover general interest topics or events, written by the publication's staff of journalists who may not have enough knowledge or experience in the field. While many articles are edited and information presented is fact checked, it may still be used incorrectly.

On the other hand, scholarly articles or academic journals are more comprehensive as they are written by scholars and researchers for academics, professionals, and experts in the field. The general public may not understand everything because these articles are longer and narrower in scope but provide in-depth analysis. These articles are even more complicated by the fact that technical or scholarly language is used, which may be too advanced for normal readers. The articles contain original research findings and other source materials are meticulously cited. Visuals-wise, you may find charts and graphs to help illustrate their findings. In addition to being edited and fact-checked, scholarly articles are peer-reviewed, meaning that panels of experts review submitted articles to ensure that the research process is valid and that the findings contribute something new to the field before finally publicizing them.

## Identifying Biases

This is one of the hardest skills to master because even the best of us have some biases they are unaware of. Being good at critical thinking involves the ability to analyze information objectively. Think of yourself as a judge and you need to evaluate the validity of the claims of both sides of an argument while keeping in mind that biases may be present in there.

It is also important to learn how to set aside your own personal biases that might cloud your judgment, and that can be a very difficult task to accomplish. Another person may be able to identify a few biases that you have and this is why the decision-making body consists of more than one individual. In this context, you want someone to argue with so that you can reach a more objective decision. If no one is available, you can only argue with yourself. That is okay too because you can still challenge your own thoughts and assumptions. That way, it is still possible to see things from different viewpoints.

To improve this area, start by challenging yourself to identify evidence that forms your beliefs. Moreover, determine whether or not your sources are credible. Most importantly, remember that bias exists. When it comes to evaluating information or an argument, consider the following:

- Who will benefit from this?
- Does the source of this information appear to have an agenda?
- Is it overlooking, ignoring, or leaving out certain information that does not support its claims?
- Is the source using wordings in a way to sway an audience's perception of a fact?

## Inference

Being able to infer and draw conclusions based on the information given is also key. The information you get does not always tell you explicitly what it means. Most of the time, you need to go through the raw data and then connect the dots on your own.

This skill allows you to extrapolate and identify potential results when assessing a scenario. Of course, because you need to use your own judgment to interpret data, the inference is not always correct. For instance, if you read that someone weighs 300 pounds, you may infer that they are overweight and unhealthy. However, when other data such as body composition and height are included, your conclusion may change.

So, how do you improve in this field? An inference is an educated guess because you try to make sense of the data you currently have. Here, your ability to infer correctly and accurately can be further enhanced by collecting as much information as possible before making conclusions. When you are faced with a new scenario or situation to evaluate, stop and try to skim for clues first. Look for things like headlines, images, features, and statistics and ask yourself what you think is going on.

## Determining Relevance

One of the hardest parts of critical thinking is when you need to figure out what information is most important for you to consider. In most cases, you will have a plethora of information that may seem important to you, although it may turn out to be only a small fraction to consider.

To improve your ability to determine the importance and relevance of data, start by establishing a clear direction in what you are trying to figure out. What do you need to do? Do you need to find a solution? Should you be identifying a trend? If you know what your end goal is, you will have a clearer picture of what is actually relevant.

Even so, having an objective does not mean that the task is going to be much easier because you do not know for sure what is truly relevant. It's worth having a physical list of the things you look for based on the level of relevance. When you know what you want to look for and what to prioritize, you will have a list that has a few obviously relevant pointers and a few, not-so-relevant ones at the bottom. Then, you can narrow down your focus on the lower-ranked topics and reevaluate its importance.

## Curiosity

It is convenient when you just sit back and take all the information presented to you at face value. But we all know how that is only going to lead to a disaster, especially when you need to make a decision at the end of the presentation. We are all born curious. Many parents can attest to the fact that children often ask them too many whys all the time. As we get older, we grow to keep that urge at bay and remain silent. While this can help us from being perceived as annoying, it prevents us from thinking critically.

Being curious is easy. Just make a conscious effort to ask open-ended questions about the things in your everyday life. From there, ask follow-up questions. This allows you to probe for more information.

# Chapter 4: Why Critical Thinking?

The question is why do we have to learn critical thinking skills? Why do we need these skills? Why do we need to become good critical thinkers? Most people will say that the skills we need to be good critical thinkers are problem-solving, creativity, analytical thinking, communication, collaboration, and accountability. Still, every single one of these skills falls under a broad umbrella which is called the critical thinking capacity. Let's take a look:

- Critical thinkers can solve problems effectively as they can logically consider all options and arrive at the best possible solutions based on the information they have.
- Creative thinking goes hand in hand with critical thinking because they require the compilation of new knowledge, simplification of ideas, and the identification of possibilities.
- Critical thinkers are analytical thinkers because they collect data and information from many sources and evaluate them from various angles. They are skilled at conceptualization, organization, and combination of knowledge.
- One of the important things of critical thinking is being able to embrace and value the opinions and views of other people. Moreover, critical thinkers always try to encourage others in constructive reflection that can help build bonds and inspire forward thinking in the team.
- Critical thinkers are excellent at communication as they are open-minded and more aware of others. Plus, their values and beliefs are shown by how well they communicate with others.
- Critical thinkers realize the usefulness of being selfless, ethical, and respectful of other cultures and belief systems. They work hard and try their best when interacting with other people.

Below is an excerpt from the World Economic Forum that describes the Future of Jobs released in 2016:

"The Fourth Industrial Revolution, which includes developments in previously disjointed fields such as artificial intelligence and machine learning, robotics, nanotechnology, 3D printing and genetics and biotechnology, will cause widespread disruption not only to business models but also to labor markets over the next five years, with enormous change predicted in the skill sets needed to thrive in the new landscape."

The world is changing rapidly and constantly. In the past, humanity was convinced that everything that could be invented had already been invented. When the computer was first made and become a household item, a 56K modem was deemed to be fast and 200MB of storage huge. However, nowadays, we even have 1TB in Smartphone storage. It shows that the world is changing and developing day by day and we did not even realize at the time that something was invented. Nothing is constant in life. Our society is evolving rapidly by the day. Certain things will grow and change completely in the blink of an eye. That is why we need to have a strong, well-developed critical thinking ability that can serve us. In order to adopt these changes, we need to develop resilience as well as critical thinking skills.

We can go back to learn from the past, 50 or 30 years ago. In order to become successful, what did we think was necessary to live our lives and become successful? It is true that what we thought was necessary and needed in the past is no longer important to us now. The usefulness of certain things has changed based on time and how we are living. In addition, the way we communicate and share our ideas has also transformed. In the past, we did not have a Smartphone and internet connection to send our messages across, but now, simply with the touch of a button, we can send the message and it takes a second. We also see each other's faces even when we are miles apart. The way we do our business and the consuming behavior of customers has also changed from generation to generation. Everything has its benefits and drawbacks. Changes brought about by technology and other events bring new problems and challenges that require you to think critically so you can cope with them.

Effective critical thinkers will think differently according to circumstances. However, after all, what we want to do is to make a decision as quickly as possible. It is just like when your car breaks down in rush hour traffic, or you are negotiating world peace. In such situations, you need to think critically. These two situations require critical thinking skills although they take place in vastly different settings with different things at stake. Still, they all require critical thinking ability and skills.

# Critical Thinking at the Workplace

Every employer wants employees who can use their logical thoughts to evaluate a situation and come up with the best solution to solve a problem. People with good critical thinking skills at the workplace can be trusted to make decisions on their own.

In recent years, critical thinking abilities are becoming important in every industry and workplace. We can demonstrate our critical thinking abilities with keywords such as analytical, problem solving, creativity, etc., in our CV and cover letter and more importantly, during the interview.

Critical thinking can be used in the workplace, and it varies from industry to industry. For example:
- If you are working in the hospital as a doctor with a case in hand, you will have to analyze the case and start to evaluate whether the patient should be treated or not.
If you are a manager in a company, you will need to analyze customer feedback and information to develop your company by training your staff.

## How to Demonstrate Skill

Firstly, you can write critical thinking keywords such as analytical, creativity, etc. in your CV. In the description of your work history, you can elaborate on the critical thinking abilities you have used in your previous workplace.

Secondly, you can also put critical thinking skills in your cover letter. You can mention one or two critical thinking skills and give some examples related to what you did previously in your last place of work.

Finally, you can show your critical skills keywords during the interview, which is the most essential step in getting a job. You can discuss with the interviewer and tell them you could solve a particular problem using critical thinking skills to fix it.

In some workplaces, they will give a test in regards to the use of critical thinking abilities. You will be given a case to solve. The interviewers are curious to know how you can use your critical thinking skills to find the best possible solution to solve the problems.

There are 5 must-have critical thinking skills:

- Analytical: Analytical skill is the ability to examine something carefully to see whether it is a problem. It helps people examine and interpret information as well as recognize the differences and similarities. People with good analytical skills often know which questions to ask to get more information from data analysis, information seeking reports, interpretations, and judgments.

- Communication: Communication is also very important because you will have to share your conclusion with your employers and colleagues once you find the best solution to the problem that the company is facing. You need to have good and effective communication skills to transfer the information and ideas found to inform your employers about what should be done in order to improve the situation. You will have to ask important questions, give assessments, seek collaborations, and explanations to express your opinions and ideas. You can successfully implement your findings by improving your interpersonal communication, giving presentations, and working in a team through verbal or written communication.

- Creativity: A certain level of creativity is often needed in critical thinking. With creativity, you might come up with good ideas and the best solution that no one has found before. Creativity may involve the creative eye. You will need to have cognitive flexibility, conceptualization, curiosity, imagination, abstract connection, and vision.

- Open-mindedness: In order to be able to think critically, you need to be able to place any assumption or judgment aside and only focus on analyzing the information you get. You have to be objective and assess the ideas without bias. Being open-minded means you have to embrace the different cultural perspectives, and be fair, humble, objective, and inclusive in your critical thinking.

- Problems-Solving: Problem-solving is vitally important in the critical thinking skills that involve analyzing a problem, generating, and implementing a solution. Then, you have to assess the success of the plan. Most employers do not just want employees who can only think about information critically, but they also need an employee who can actually come up with practical solutions.

## Critical Thinking in College

Throughout your years in schools and college, critical thinking is hardly used even though one can never stress its importance enough. This is one of the reasons why so many students struggle when they get into the professional world. Many of them had a completely wrong attitude toward tackling a challenging problem, and life as a whole. Such attitudes include:

- Ignorant certainty. It is the belief that all questions have definite and correct answers. This is what most students believe. In many exams, questions have a clear answer, but that is not the case in real life. There is often a grey area between the white and black. Most meaningful questions do not have a straightforward answer. In some courses, we need to think critically about the material during our study. Unfortunately, many students neglect this area.

- Naïve relativism: It is the belief that all arguments are equal and there is no truth. According to Roberts, this is a view that students tend to follow when they learn about the error of ignorant certainty. One part of critical thinking is to evaluate the validity of the argument, both your own argument and others'. Thus, we have to understand that in critical thinking, some arguments are better and some are awful.

In addition, critical thinking also allows students to form their own opinions and participate actively with the material more than just with the superficial level. In class, it is important to learn with your professors or classmates through meaningful discussion. If you just learn what is written in the book, you will never get far. Furthermore, critical thinking skills also allow you to come up with good, worthy arguments and use them to back up your ideas and opinions. If you plan to pursue higher education, original and critical thoughts are essential. As critical thinking involves evaluating information, it will also help you assess your own work. As a student, we all want better grades and good habits of mind. Without critical thinking, while you are in college, you will get somewhere, but you are not likely to be in a place where you desire.

# Critical Thinking in the Real World

Critical thinking plays a very important role in the real world and it does not stop in college. The reason is:

- Critical thinking helps you develop intellectually throughout your life even after you graduate. Graduation does not mean that you should stop learning. If anything, it is only the first step in your learning process, as there is so much more to learn out there. The world is changing and you need to keep learning as much as you can to keep yourself relevant. When faced with new challenges and information, being able to think critically will help you evaluate and use it.

- Critical thinking will help you to make difficult decisions. In a decision-making process, it is hard to make an immediate decision when you have the ability to evaluate many available options. Critical thinking will allow you to compare the pros and cons of each option and you will have more options than you can think of.

- People will take advantage of you if you let others think for you, and judge everything at face value. You may be familiar with many advertisements whose promises seem too good to be true. The useless and harmful products they sell rely on the ignorance or false hope of buyers. When you have the ability to think critically, you can avoid getting caught and motivated to buy something from unethical companies and people.

- Critical thinking will also help increase your employment rate with better pay. A good employer will not only look for an employee who can find a solution to an existing problem but will also look for someone who can come up with the best solution to the problem that no one has thought of. To get a well-paying job, you will need critical thinking skills and ability after your graduation because it is a crucial ingredient to fixing problems and difficulties.

# Chapter 5: Practical Ways to Improve Critical Thinking

In this chapter, we will go over some of the most practical ways you can improve your critical thinking skills.

## Critical Thinking Exercise

The idea of real critical thinking exercise is to find the truth. It requires us to move away from traditional thinking in order to find the truth.

Critical thinking is like a muscle. It takes constant practice to improve it. Thinking criticallyand gathering knowledge and experience. How can we keep improving our critical thinking skills? How can we encourage people to continue improving their critical thinking skills for a lifetime?

Improving our critical thinking does not need hours of lesson planning or require special materials. Thinking critically yields many benefits but you just need to be curious and open-minded. Below are some strategies you can employ to help you improve your critical thinking skills in your everyday life.

There is no magical way to immediately improve our critical thinking, and it will take time to practice in a regular way.

## Don't Waste Time

Have you ever noticed that when you waste time you get nothing out of it? It is true that everyone has had this experience in their lives, even those who are good critical thinkers. It is like nature where water waste and time waste is unavoidable. Many people have not used their time productively and sometimes, not even pleasurably. Thankfully, we can maximize productivity and minimize time wasted on trivial matters. For instance, you can take the time you would spend watching TV to plan your days ahead.

We have arranged some questions that you can use to review how you practice your thinking throughout the day:

- When did I make my worst thinking today? When did I make my best thinking?
- What kind of things did I spend time thinking about today?
- Did I figure out something from my thinking?
- Did I permit negative thoughts to frustrate me easily?
- If I had a chance to repeat my day, what would I want to do differently? Why?
- Did I do anything that benefits my long term goals?
- If I spent time thinking the same way as I did today for 10 years, would I have achieved something important in my life at that time?

You need to spend more time going through all of them or just a few in order to carefully and internally think about your response and record it in your journal. The more you spend time practicing this, the better you will be and you will see more patterns emerging in your thinking habits.

## Learn Something New Every Day

Continuing to learn for a lifetime is all about making the process of learning an ongoing journey. We just need to learn something new that we did not know before. You can start by asking yourself what you have been curious to know. Is there a question about something that you want to get an answer for? If so, go and chase it. Do not stop till you figure out the answer you are looking for. No matter how simple or unimportant the question might be to other people. Just do not take that into account. From this practice, you can accomplish two things at the same time. One is, you can fulfill your intellectual needs and second, you can develop your habit of curiosity.

## No Boundaries for Learning

Never ever think that you are too old to learn something new or achieve something amazing. There are many famous people who have accomplished great things when they are old, so ignore your age and start learning something new. There is no age restriction for learning, particularly, in the process of improving critical thinking skills.

# Always Question

Asking questions shows a sign of intelligence. Asking questions means you are curious to know more. In today's world, we should encourage our children to ask more questions to discover possibilities and opportunities. Questions are good and good questions are better. The core of critical thinking and lifelong learning is the ability to ask meaningful questions that can lead to constructive and useful answers. Encouraging people to learn with asking questions as the focus will ensure that we and our learners do not learn in one way. It is a highly interactive learning process when we exchange ideas and discuss through asking questions. As a result, we can develop a habit of curiosity by asking questions to look for other opinions and views, taking nothing for granted.

The following questions are used to improve critical thinking skills: Think of something that you have just been told by someone and after that ask yourself the questions below:
- Who?
  - Do you know that person?
  - Is that person in power?
  - Is it important to know who told you this?

- What?
  - Is it a fact or an opinion?
  - Are all the facts provided?
  - Is there anything left out?

- Where?
  - Public or private?
  - Were you given a chance to respond?

- When?
  - Is there any reason for their opinion?
  - Are they trying to make someone look good or bad?

- - How?
- Happy, sad or angry?
- Spoken or written?
- Could you understand?

## Active Listening

Active listening is really essential in critical thinking as you will have enough information from the speaker and by paying attention, you will come up with good questions that lead to getting more information. Some say that you have two ears and a mouth for a reason. A good listener lets others talk first before expressing his or her own ideas and opinions. According to a study from the University of Missouri, many people are weak listeners. It does not help when there are so many distractions, either. Most people think that listening is an easy thing to do, but it is actually very difficult, especially for active listening. In order to be an active listener, we need to have a conscious and concerted effort to hear words being said by the speakers and more importantly, we have to understand what is being said in their message. Moreover, it is also crucial to understand what the speaker wants or is striving to achieve in the conversation.

### Improving Active Listening

Active listening skills like other communication skills can be learned, accomplished, and taught.

**Talk less**: This should be obvious because it is impossible to both talk and listen at the same time. Listen and do not try to talk or think of a reply just yet. Focus on what the speaker is saying to get a clear message. After that, you can respond. That way, you allow the speaker to say all that needs to be said so you can fully understand what they are trying to say.

**Adopt a listening mode**: Keep silent and pay attention to hear what they are saying. Furthermore, keep the environment quiet and open your mind in a comfortable manner with engaging eye contact. At the same time, make sure you are responding appropriately. Active listening is meant to promote respect and understanding. When listening, you gain more information, data, perspective, and insights. Attacking the speaker now and putting them down does not help anyone. Of course, that does not mean you should just sit there and nod, either. This brings us to the next point.

**Respond properly:** Be candid, honest, and open in your response and assert your opinions respectfully. When you respond and provide your own opinions, keep in mind that yours can sound just as wrong to them as theirs to you. Remember what is important in the discussion: reaching an agreement on the best solution. So, it does not matter who is right. What matters here is that a good decision has been made that day. Plus, you are here to take in ideas and knowledge and the other person is there to share it. You can save the discussion until after the presentation. There will always be an opportunity to talk.

**Make the Speaker Feel Comfortable**: You have to show some gestures or signs of agreement in your listening. If you think that seating makes you both feel comfortable, you can arrange the seat for the conversation. Be aware of the environment in which you are communicating.

**Avoid Distraction**: This means you have to make sure that you keep your phone in silent mode, keep the TV screen or speaker off. If the speakers request privacy, you can hold the conversation in a private room and close the door.

**Put Your Personal Prejudice Aside**: It is difficult for most people, but we can tackle this issue through learning and practice. Interrupting people is considered rude and a waste of time because it only serves to infuriate the speaker and restricts a full understanding of the message. Therefore, allow the speaker to finish each point properly. In some cases, the speaker will pause, offering you the opportunity to ask a question. That is the time to speak. Also, never interrupt with a counter-argument.

**Pay Attention to Their Tone**: The tone of the speaker's words can sometimes enhance the meaning of the words and sometimes, it can hide the meaning of the words. Make sure, you know the difference.

**Look for the Underlying Meaning**: In our listening, we will hear words, of course, but it is not something we want to listen. What we want to listen to is the underlying meaning, not really the words. Therefore, at first, we have to listen for comprehension and second, for ideas.

**Pay Attention to Non-verbal Language**: People do not only communicate through verbal language, but they can also use body language and facial expressions. That is why it is important that we use eye contact in our conversation

**Provide feedback:** Sometimes, we may misunderstand what the speaker is trying to say because of our personal biases, assumptions, judgments, and beliefs. Listening actively means that you need to understand what is being said as intended by the speaker. To achieve this, simply paraphrase what is being said. Put what they said into your own words and confirm with the speaker whether you got their message right. If you do not quite get what the speaker is trying to say, ask clarifying questions. Moreover, summarize the speaker's comments now and again to confirm that the two of you are still on the same page.

## Solve Just the Problem

As human beings, we have got so many problems at hand and little time to solve them. These problems can be at the workplace, at home, or in society. Problems that we create through our action and choice or happen independently without our influence do not go away on their own. The only thing that we can do is to solve them on one by one, one day at a time. Hopefully, we can avoid these problems in the future.

You can start solving a problem in one day, every day so that you can keep your focus on it with undivided focus.

You can consider the words of author and speaker Les Brown "If you've got a problem that either man or god can solve, then you ain't got no problem." So, there is no need to be worried about facing problems at all. They are inevitable and we can achieve more if we embrace and see them as the mundane things in life. We can move on to solve them with a positive attitude.

Now, let's take a look at one approach mapped out by authors Richard Paul and Linda Elder. In their approach, you will have the roadmap to solving a problem you want to face daily.

- You have to state the problem as clearly and precisely as you can.
- You have to understand your problem and know what you are dealing with, and you also need to put aside the other problems that you have no control over which saves you time to focus on the problem that you can actually solve.
- You need to figure out the information you need and actively discover it.
- You need to analyze and interpret the information you collect carefully.
- You need to also identify what you can do in the short term and long term. Figure out all the options for action and visualize the most appropriate solution you want to achieve.
- You have to evaluate your options, and take into account their pros and cons.
- You have to take up a strategic approach to the problem and follow through with it.
- You need to track your progress as you implement your actions and be ready to review and alter your strategy should the need arise. Plus, your strategy should be flexible enough to allow changes when more information is available to you.

Through all these five practices, it takes lots of time and practice to improve our critical thinking skills. In addition, you will see significant improvement of your critical thinking skills when you follow all of these simple activities and systems.

## Improving Critical Thinking Every Day

Now you already know what critical thinking is and the steps and ways you can improve critical thinking, but what we want to talk about in this section is how we can keep practicing and improving our critical thinking skills. You will find practical and beneficial ways to keep improving your skills, and as you practice these ways every day, on and on, you will feel comfortable with critical thinking in your daily life.

As human beings, we are great and have the capacity to do almost anything. However, we tend not to make use of those capacities and live undeveloped. Improving critical thinking is like improving in any other aspect like in sports. Improvement is not likely to happen if there is no conscious commitment to learn and practice. If we take our thinking for granted, you will see nothing improve. It takes time for the development of critical thinking, and the result will not come overnight. It will develop gradually over time. How can we develop as critical thinkers? How can we keep improving and practicing over time in everyday life?

We have to understand that there are phases needed in developing our critical thinking skills

Phase1: The Unreflective Thinkers: they are not aware of the problems they are having in their thinking.

Phase2: The Challenged Thinkers; they know what problems they are having in their thinking.

Phase3: The Beginning Thinkers; they try to improve their thinking, but do not practice on a regular basis.

Phase4: The Practicing Thinkers; they begin to realize the necessity of regular practice.

Phase5: The Advanced Thinkers; they start to advance their thinking together with their regular practice.

Phase6: The Master Thinker: they are skilled at critical thinking that it becomes their habit to think critically.

## How to Sharpen Your Logical Thinking Skills

We all know about Sherlock and his unparalleled logical thinking skills. Thankfully, this is something that we can all achieve with a little practice.

Of course, maybe a convoluted murder case is out of your league, but at least you can improve your logical thinking skills to a level that makes problem-solving and decision-making much easier. These skills will contribute to success in your personal and professional life. So, what can you do to sharpen your mind?

### Learn the Terminology

Before you start brushing up on your logical thinking skills, it is worth knowing its set of terms and being acquainted with them. That way, the rest of the journey will be much easier.

You need to know terms such as premise, assumption, conclusion, argument, observation, inference, various types of statement, etc.

## Making Logical Conclusions

It does sound strange, but practice makes perfect. You do not need to get yourself into a difficult situation to improve your logical thinking skills. Trying to think in conditional statements and find causes and consequences of small and insignificant facts is enough. Basically, just identify the premise and conclusion in any conditional statement and establish a link between them.

For example, let us assume that if it is raining, it is cold outside. So, we have the statement: "If it is raining, it is cold outside." In a conditional sentence, if the premise is true, then the conclusion is also true. That's it. Just develop this kind of thinking with other things and see if the relationship works between the premise and conclusion.

## Play Card Games

There are other ways to make the learning process fun. Why not gather your friends once every week to play a light-hearted card game to stimulate your brain to think quickly and logically? Challenging card games will only dampen the mood and make the learning process arduous. Simple card games help improve your memory, focus, and analytical skills.

You can even incorporate strategy into these games to spice things up. Games such as Crazy Eight or Go Fish are perfect for kids. For adults, games such as Black Jack or Poker work just as well.

## Make Math Fun

Okay, math is one of the least fun things in the world, but it is also one of the best exercises to improve your logical thinking skills. It is unappealing to both adults and children, and even less so as a pastime activity. But hear us out. You see, math is more than just crunching of numbers. Those who excel in math are actually fluent in logic because the only difference between the two is numbers and letters. Math is logic simplified so everyone can make sense of it.

Thankfully, you do not need to sit and crunch numbers all evening to improve your logical thinking skills. There are plenty of fun ways to work on your math. There are plenty of mental challenges in math games on many websites or mobile phone apps that you can access.

Other math-related games such as Sudoku are also engaging and challenging, allowing you to improve your brain's ability to solve real problems faster.

**Solve Mysteries and Break Codes**

Another way to make learning logical thinking is by reading crime stories and detective novels. They require logical thinking from readers, after all. If reading is not your cup of tea, consider watching movies or TV shows in that genre instead. The challenge here is to solve the mystery before the hero of the story does. Of course, there will be plot twists or different interpretations of evidence, so do not be discouraged if it is actually different from what you had imagined. What matters here is you get yourself to think logically.

In this case, you often have many possibilities. Your work here is to eliminate those that are improbable or impossible. Another great brain exercise is Breaking Codes, which you can find on the internet and play with your friend.

**Debate**

Debates challenge us to string our thoughts together in a convincing way. While we know something is good or bad, explaining that to others is difficult. Debates force us to search for causes and consequences behind our beliefs, and turn them into strong arguments and find the logical connection behind everything.

Because you need to think logically and decide on the fly, debates can improve your logical thinking skills. So, join a debate club or organize a debate with your friends about literature, society, music, politics, etc.

**Be Strategic**

Logical thinking is all about understanding logical connections and putting the pieces together. By learning how to think strategically, you will develop a valuable asset for both your personal and professional life. Strategic thinking habits include anticipating, critical thinking, interpreting, deciding, and learning. You can improve this kind of thinking by playing strategic games such as board games, or video games, or design a strategy for sports events.

**Notice the Pattern**

Individuals with great logical thinking skills see patterns that others might otherwise miss every day. These patterns test their logical reasoning skills and how they anticipate and complete them. A great way to train pattern recognition is by scrutinizing everything and finding an answer through an educated guess.

For example, we have a string of numbers: 1, 4, 9, 16, and 25. Which of the below follows?

a. 50
b. 36
c. 44
d. 78

If you chose B, then congratulations. You noticed the pattern in the numbers. Each number in the string is squared and goes up by one. So, it's 1x1, 2x2, 3x3, 4x4, and 5x5. You need to familiarize yourself with these problems to quickly think of an answer.

# 7 Ways to Think More Critically

"Thinking is skilled work. It is not true that we are naturally endowed with the ability to think clearly and logically-without learning how, or without practicing" A.E. Mander.

## Ask Simple Questions

Does every complicated thing need a complicated solution? Sometimes, we give too much explanation until we almost get lost or forget the original question. In order to avoid this, we will have to go back to the basic questions you asked for solving the problem. These basic questions include:

- What do you already know?
- How do you know this?
- What are you trying to prove, show, and criticize...?

- What do you miss looking at?

## Question Basic Assumption

It is easy to make you look like a fool simply by not questioning your basic assumption. In the past, many scientific breakthroughs started by challenging commonly held beliefs. Those innovators in our history just looked up and said: "What if we're wrong?" If you want to make it happen in reality, you just question your assumption and think critically about what is appropriate and possible.

## Know Your Mental Processes

What puts us above other animals is our ability to think. Unfortunately, thinking critically is not always easy because of the way and how we think. Our brain tends to use a mental shortcut to explain what is going on around us. The mental shortcut can be useful when you are in a situation where you have to make a quick decision such as when you are hunting large game and fighting off wild animals. However, it can be a problem when you are trying to make a decision that may affect your life. This is because these shortcuts are not always accurate. That is why it is critical to be aware of your own cognitive biases and personal prejudice as they both influence our decisions.

It is true that we as human beings have biases in our thinking, but to be aware of it is what makes critical thinking possible and something that a good critical thinker needs to take into account.

## Try Reversing Things

A great way to avoid deadlock in a difficult problem is to try reversing things in a different way. It is obvious that X comes from Y, but what if Y comes from X?

A popular story that people always raise is the chicken and egg story. It is a good example to show in this case. At first, it is obvious that the chicken comes first before the egg because chickens lay eggs. However, we can also ask where the chicken comes from. It must be from somewhere. Since the chicken comes from an egg, it is true that the egg comes before the chicken, right?

Sometimes, we all know that the reverse is not true, but at least it can help you set out the right path to arrive at the best solution to the problem.

## Evaluate the Existing Evidence

It is useful to review the previous work done in the past on the same topic when we are trying to solve a problem. Moreover, it is essential to evaluate the information we gain critically, or otherwise, we will reach a wrong conclusion. You can simply start by asking simple questions. For example, who collected this evidence and how did he or she do it? Why did he or she do it?

For example, one study shows that sugary cereal has health benefits. On paper, this study sounds quite persuasive. However, when you think critically and try to find out more about it, it shows that a cereal company funded the study. Thus, more or less, the company may influence the finding of the study.

However, we cannot assume automatically that the result of the study is invalid, but we have to keep in mind that we should be aware of a conflict of interest.

## Remember to Think for Yourself

Some people do not trust in themselves and only rely on research or reading. They forget to think for themselves which is sometimes the most powerful tool. We should not be overconfident, but we have to understand that thinking for ourselves is really needed in responding to difficult questions. This simply happens when you are writing essays. It is so easy for most people to get lost in someone else's work that they forget to use their own thoughts, opinions, and ideas.

## No One Can Think Critically 100% of the Time

It is important to understand that no one can continually think critically all the time. It is totally fine. Still, critical thinking should be employed when you need to make major decisions or solve complicated problems. However, there is no need to think critically about everything. During the decision-making process of an important decision, sometimes we will experience a lapse in our reasoning, but we just need to recognize it and try to get away from it in the future.

## Ways to Improve Our Critical Thinking

Critical thinking is just the way that we process information deliberately and systematically so that we can make good decisions and understand things better.

There are some ways to think about information critically. These include:

- Conceptualizing
- Analyzing
- Synthesizing
- Evaluating

The information that we want to think of critically can come from different sources such as through:

- Observation
- Experience
- Reflection
- Reasoning
- Communication

All of these sources will guide us to believe and take action.

Critical thinking is not like how we regularly think every day. In a certain moment, we happen to think automatically, but when we think deliberately, we will use some of the critical thinking tools and skills to reach more accurate conclusions than we normally would every day.

Most of our thinking every day is not critical, and that's good for us because we do not have to spend a lot of our brain energy to think about everything. If we had to think about everything critically or deliberately, we would not have any cognitive energy left to think about something else that is more important. Thus, it is good that much of our everyday thinking happens automatically.

However, we can run into problems if we let our automatic mental process govern important decisions. If we do not have critical thinking skills, it is easy for people to control us. In our everyday life, if we fail to stop and think deliberately, it is easy for us to get caught up in pointless arguments or involved in silly things.

# Chapter 6: How to Implement Critical Thinking

In this chapter, we will look at how you can implement critical thinking into your everyday life by following a few practical steps and thinking processes. Without further ado, let us get into this.

## 6 Steps for Effective Critical Thinking

We have to deal with problems on a day-to-day basis, from small and insignificant things to major, life-changing decisions. In many cases, we are challenged to understand a different perspective when we approach any situation. Our thought process is based on previous experience or similar situations. While that allows us to think quickly, that does not always mean we can solve problems effectively because our judgment may be clouded by our emotions. Not only that, our decisions may be further affected by prioritizing the wrong factors, or other external factors as well. Here, critical thinking allows us to establish a rational, open-minded decision-making process that is based mainly on solid facts and evidence.

As we have mentioned earlier, we have developed some mental shortcuts that help us make decisions quicker, especially during life-or-death situations. Here, critical thinking prevents us from jumping straight into conclusions. It may slow down our thought process, but it helps us in making the right decision. It helps guide us through logical steps that allow us to discover more perspectives and solutions while removing those mental shortcuts that are based on personal biases. The critical thinking process has six steps:

**Knowledge**

Every problem requires a clear vision to see the right solution. In this step, you need to identify the problem. To do so, ask a lot of questions to understand every little thing about the scenario. That way, you can understand what influences the outcome or what you need to address from the start. In some cases, there is no actual problem so no need to go forward with other steps. This is just as important because trying to solve a problem that does not exist is a waste of time and may worsen the situation. To identify the problem, start by asking open-ended questions to gather as much information as possible and pave the way for discussion and explore the problem. The two main questions to be asked are: What is the problem? Why do we need to solve it?

**Comprehension**

After identifying the situation, you can then try to understand the facts and circumstances that led up to this moment. The information gathering process should follow any of the research methods that can be changed according to the problem, the type of data available, and the deadline required to solve it.

**Application**

Continuing on from the previous step, this step requires you to connect the dots from the information you gathered to the resources available to solve the problem. You can use mind maps to assist you in analyzing the situation, establishing a relation between it and the core problem, and determining the best approach to proceed.

**Analyze**

When all the data is collected and connections have been made between it and the main issues, the situation is thoroughly assessed to identify what is really going on, the pros and cons, and the challenges involved in solving the problem. You should focus on the root causes and think of how you can address them in the solution. You can use a cause-effect diagram to help you analyze the problem and its circumstances. The diagram helps you divide the problem from its causes, identify and categorize them based on their types and impact on the problem.

**Synthesis**

After the problem is fully analyzed and all the relevant information is considered, the next step would be to decide how to solve the problem and create an action plan. If there is more than one solution, their advantages and drawbacks should be considered. Identify what you prioritize to find the best solution in your interest. We recommend you use SWOT analysis to identify the solution's strengths, weaknesses, opportunities, and threats.

**Action**

The final step is to put your decision into action. Critical thinking also applies in the action phase and the action should have its own steps. If your action plan is long-term or involves a team, it is worth having an action plan to help you execute your decision properly.

Moreover, your plan should have certain indicators to identify how well the work is going so you can evaluate your progress and adapt as needed. Of course, your action plan should be clear but flexible.

## Asking the Right Questions

Critical thinking is about utilizing the information that you have to the best of your ability. As such, it is just as important to gather the right kind of information. One way to do that is either by observation or questioning. Observation can only get you so far as it can only answer some of the most basic questions.

Asking the right questions allows you to understand the situation better and analyze it properly. There are so many questions to ask, but you can follow the Starbursting method by asking the 6 questions: How, what, where, when, why, and who?

For example, suppose that you are tasked with solving an accessibility problem at your office. There have been complaints about the fact that certain stairs placement has made it difficult for disabled people to gain access to some areas, particularly the main entrance as it is slightly elevated, requiring the use of stairs. So, the questions you should ask first are:

- Who: Who is intended to use the stairs?
- What: What is wrong with the stairs? What are the options to solve the problem?
- How: How can we implement our options? How can we design the stairs in a way that disabled people can use?
- Where: Where will we use these new ideas?
- When: When do disabled people use the stairs the most?
- Why: Why do we need to change the stars' design? Why do disabled people have such a bad experience?

Alternatively, you can also use the elements of thoughts to help you identify the right questions. Elements of thoughts reflect how we think about the situation. They include purpose, questions, information, interpretation, concepts, assumptions, implications, and points of view.

- Purpose: Goals and objectives. The question: What are we trying to solve? What do I want to achieve?
- Question: Problems and issues. The question: What should I need to ask?

- Information: Data, facts, observations, experiences. The question: What do I need to know to understand the problem?
- Interpretation: Conclusions and solutions. The question: How do others come up with different solutions?
- Concepts: Definitions, theories, laws, principles, and models. The question: What is the main concept of this idea?
- Assumptions: Presuppositions and axioms. The question: What are we assuming to be true or false without confirming them?
- Implications: Results and consequences. The question: How can we implicate these new ideas?
- Point of view: Frames of reference, perspectives, orientations. The question: How are the different points of view related to the problem?

The next step, of course, is to answer all the questions without any assumptions or prejudices. Here, you should have a deep understanding of the problem and you can move forward with the steps needed to find the best solution to the problem. In our example here, the solution includes using elevators in places where disabled people can easily find and access them or using sloped platforms to allow wheelchair users to go up and down easily.

## SWOT Analysis

SWOT analysis is a great tool to use, in this context, to understand the strengths, weaknesses, opportunities, and threats of a solution or situation. SWOT analysis provides a systematic way of analyzing a solution to your problem. Understanding what the pros and cons are and knowing what you should prioritize is key to identifying an optimal solution. It can be used either as an icebreaker to get people into the strategy formulation process or as a strategy tool.

### Strengths

Here, you should consider both internal and external perspectives when evaluating the viability of a solution. If you have problems identifying strengths, try to make a list of the characteristics of a solution or situation. That way, you may be able to identify a few of them as strengths. Questions should include:

- What does this have that others do not?
- What advantage does the situation provide?

## Weaknesses

Just like the previous element, also consider your weaknesses from both an internal and external perspective. It is best to be realistic and acknowledge any unpleasant facts as soon as possible. Be honest with yourself. Questions should include:

- What should you avoid?
- How is this solution or situation lacking?

## Opportunities

A good way to analyze opportunities is to determine if their strengths open up any opportunities. If not, then look at their weaknesses and try to identify what you can get by eliminating them.

## Threats

Threats mainly focus on the obstacles that hold you back from achieving your goal and evaluate how serious your weaknesses are.

Another good analysis tool called PEST analysis can help you identify opportunities and threats, ensuring that you do not overlook external factors such as government regulations or technological development.

# PEST Analysis

PEST analysis is mainly used in the organizational context to help identify opportunities and threats in the business environment. For instance, you can reach new customers through new technologies, which is identified as an opportunity. On the other hand, threats can be the shrinking market, increased interest rates, or intensified competition thanks to deregulation.

PEST analysis helps you take external factors into consideration such as political, economic, socio-cultural, and technological changes in your business environment. That way, you have a better picture of the bigger forces that you are exposed to and take advantage of the opportunities that arise from them.

The difference between PEST analysis and SWOT analysis is that the former focuses on the larger factors that are often outside our domain of control such as the economy, technology, and government. The latter is a narrower scope, focusing only on the organization or individual. We recommend you use these two when you need to make major decisions as they complement each other very well.

PEST analysis comes in many names, and they are all abbreviations of what you need to consider:

- PESTLE/PESTEL: Political, economic, socio-cultural, technological, legal, and environmental
- LONGPESTLE: Local, national, and global version of PESTLE. It is best used to understand changes in a multinational organization.
- SLEPT: Socio-cultural, legal, economic, political, and technological.
- PESTLIED: Political, economic, socio-cultural, technological, legal, international, environmental, and demographic.
- STEEPLE: Socio/Demographic, technological, economic, environmental, political, legal, and ethical.

PEST analysis has four main reasons for its use:

- It helps you identify personal or business opportunities and it helps you perceive significant threats in advance.
- It identifies the changes needed in an organization or within your business environment. It also helps you shape what you are doing so you can work to achieve the desired change rather than against it.
- It helps prevent you from starting a project that is doomed to fail for reasons outside your control.
- It can help you identify and eliminate certain assumptions that you unconsciously make when you enter a new country, region, or market by developing an objective view of this unfamiliar environment.

Using this tool is pretty straightforward. All you need to do is brainstorm all the changes happening around you and the opportunities and threats that may come from these changes. From there, decide on which action to take.

**Brainstorming**

There are four main factors to consider: political, economic, socio-cultural, and technological factors.

**Political Factors**

Ask yourself the following questions:

- Could any pending legislation or taxation changes affect your business? If so, how?
- Are there any political factors that may change in the near future?
- What is the timescale of proposed legislative changes?
- How does the government view corporate policy, corporate social responsibility, environmental issues, and customer protection legislation? What can these factors change? Are they likely to change?
- How developed are the property rights and the rule of law?
- How widespread are corruption and organized crime?
- When is the next local, state, or national election? How can this influence government or regional policy?
- Who is the most likely winner for power? What are their views on business policy and other policies that affect your organization?

**Economic Factors**
- How stable is the country's economy? Is it declining, stagnating, or growing?
- Are customers' levels of disposable income rising or falling? How likely is that to change in a few years?
- What is the unemployment rate? How easy is it to find a skilled workforce? How expensive is it to hire a skilled workforce?

- Are the exchange rates stable or do they fluctuate wildly?
- How is globalization influencing the economic environment?
- Do consumers and businesses have access to credit? If not, how will this affect your business?
- Are there any other economic factors you need to consider?

**Socio-Cultural Factors**
- What are the population's beliefs and lifestyle choices? How will they affect the population and your organization?
- What social attitudes and social taboos are present in that environment? How could they affect your business? Have there been any socio-cultural changes that affect this?
- What employment patterns, attitudes toward work, and job market trends can you identify? Are they different for different age groups?
- What is the population's growth rate and age profile? How likely is it to change?
- What are society's levels of social mobility, education, and health? Are they changing? How? What impact do they have?
- Will generation shifts in attitude affect your business?

**Technological Factors**
- Are there any new technologies you can use to boost your organization's performance?
- Are there any new upcoming technologies that can affect the business environment?
- Do your competitors have access to new technologies that can give them an advantage?
- In which areas do government and educational institutions focus their research? How can you take advantage of this?
- Are there any existing technological hubs you can work with or learn from?
- How have infrastructure changes affected your work patterns such as levels of remote working?
- Are there any other technological factors you should be aware of?

## Opportunities

From the extensive list of what you have gathered from the previous PEST analysis, you can then proceed to study each change and how it can pave the way for new opportunities for you. For instance, can it help you develop new products, assess new markets, or make the production process more efficient?

### Threats

It is just as important to understand how the changes can negatively affect your business. If you identify the threats early enough, you may be able to avoid them or at least minimize their impact.

For instance, if a new piece of technology is threatening your business, what can you do about it to improve the product instead? If your target market is in demographic decline, what other areas of the market can you access?

### Action

Finally, after identifying major opportunities and threats, establishing an action plan to exploit opportunities and manage or eliminate risks, can then put your plans into action. As always, make sure your plan is not too rigid. You need to establish indicators to tell how well you are doing. If things are not going well, then you should be able to identify what went wrong and how you can change your plan. Evaluate, rinse, and repeat.

## The Six Thinking Hats

Your thinking style has its own pros and cons. Optimistic thinkers often see the chances but tend to overlook the risks or downsides associated with them. Cautious thinkers are the opposite, seeing only risks and not opportunities. By changing up your thinking style, you may be able to find new solutions to tricky problems.

The best way to approach a problem is by viewing it from various angles. You can use the "Six Thinking Hats" model to help you adopt different viewpoints. It can also be used as a decision-checking tool in group situations because you can encourage everyone to explore the situation from many perspectives simultaneously.

By forcing you to move away from your habitual style of thinking, the Six Thinking Hats model allows you to look at a situation from a different perspective, allowing you to view a situation more objectively.

While you can think up a good solution to your problem using a rational, positive viewpoint, it is still worth exploring the problem from other angles. For instance, you can view the problem from an intuitive, creative, emotional, or risk management viewpoint. You may be surprised to see what good solutions you are missing out on. Plus, not deciding these can mean making a decision that is poorly received by others because their needs are not met, creative ideas are not used, or essential contingency plans are not acknowledged.

**How to Implement the Six Thinking Hats Model**

The Six Thinking Hats model can be used in meetings by assigning everyone to every hat evenly, or on your own. In a meeting, it has the added benefit of confrontation prevention because when everyone is viewing the problem from different angles, all their opinions are valid. As you may have already guessed, each thinking hat is a way of thinking.

**White Hat**

White Hat is a thinking style that primarily focuses on the available data. You look at what information you have, analyze past trends, and try to spot a pattern or learn something from it. Try to find gaps in your knowledge and try to account for them or fill them. It is important that you do not proceed further than comprehending the facts and knowledge gap. The questions here are: "What do we know?" and "What is the data that we have?"

**Red Hat**

Red hat focuses more on intuition, gut feeling, and emotion. Think of this for you and those affected by your decisions. Most importantly, try to understand the responses coming from those who do not understand your reasoning. The objective of this thinking style is to understand the emotional reaction from everyone but not try to understand the reason behind those reactions. Here, you should ask "What do you feel about this suggestion?" and "Does anything feel off to you?"

**Black Hat**

Black hat thinking focuses mainly on the negative outcomes of any decision. Wearing this hat, you need to look at everything cautiously and defensively. Instead of seeing how it could work, see where it could go wrong. This is critical as it highlights any weak points in a plan, allowing you to eliminate, alter, or prepare contingency plans to counter them.

This style of thinking helps you build a more solid plan because you spot fatal flaws and risks before you implement the plan, which would be too late by then as you may have already sunk resources into it. Many successful people are often over-optimistic about their situation, which tends to leave them vulnerable as they cannot see problems in advance. This makes them unprepared for difficulties. You should ask the following questions: "What are the risks?" and "How can this go wrong?"

**Yellow Hat**

This is a positive way of thinking. The yellow represents hope as it is the color of the sun. You adopt an optimistic viewpoint to help you discover all the benefits of your decisions and the values in them. Yellow Hat thinking often serves to motivate you when the going gets tough. The questions to be asked here are: "What are the advantages of implementing this solution?" and "Why do you think this is viable?"

**Green Hat**

The color green represents intelligence. In this context, it represents creativity. Wearing this hat, you need to think of creative approaches to a problem. This is a free way of thinking where there is little criticism of ideas.

**Blue Hat**

This style of thinking focuses mainly on process control. It is intended to guide the whole decision-making process and determine which thinking that everyone should use. For instance, when ideas are running dry, they may focus on Green Hat thinking. When things go wrong and contingency plans are needed, Black Hat thinking will be used.

**An Example of Six Hats**

So, how do these go together in a real-life situation? All of them can be applied to different scenarios based on the aim of the decision. Moreover, you can also use this thinking model in an educational context to help students develop creative thinking skills and learn how to identify solutions based on an in-depth understanding of the problems. We have two examples for you. In the first example, different people wear different Thinking Hats. In the second example, everyone wears the same Thinking Hat and then changes throughout the decision-making process.

**Example 1:** Suppose that you are one of the directors of a property company. The board of directors is considering whether they should build a new office block. From a glance, everyone can tell that the economy is flourishing and there is a high demand for vacant office spaces as they are being bought left, right, and center. So, how does the Six Thinking Hat model fit into the decision-making process?

Starting with the White Hat, everyone looks at the data they have. They see that their supply, which is vacant office space in the city, is going down. If they decide to build a new office building now, the existing office space should be in extremely short supply by the time the new building block is finished. You also know that the economy is growing and steady growth is expected to continue.

Then, thinking with the Red Hat, some directors may say that the current building design looks gloomy and old. They may say that people may find the working environment unappealing from the design and want it changed.

Looking at the Black Hat thinkers, they ponder whether the economic forecast may be wrong. If the economy were to suddenly experience a downturn, many office buildings would sit empty or only partly occupied for a long time. Suddenly, the company is looking at an economy with high supply and low demand. Not only that, the Red Hat thinkers point out the aesthetic flaw of the office design, so other companies will only buy office buildings that are more attractive.

On the other spectrum, the Yellow Hat thinkers know that there are risks associated with investing in the construction of another office building block. They point out that, suppose the economy is still doing well and their projections are correct, and then they have much to gain as the company can make a hearty profit. Even if they were to suffer an economic downturn, perhaps they could sell their buildings before then, or rent them out on long-term leases that could last through any recession, which makes purchasing their buildings an appealing prospect for many businesses even if the buildings themselves are not as pleasing to the eyes.

The Green Hat thinkers took the advice from the Red Hat, Yellow Hat, and Black Hat thinkers and consider whether they should redesign the building to make it more appealing. They have a few options to consider here. They can either build prestige offices that people would want to rent regardless of the economic climate. They can also wait until the economic downturn happens, which would drive down office building costs. Then, they can invest the money into buying those properties, selling them after the economy is flourishing again.

Finally, the Blue Hat thinkers control the whole process, ensuring that the discussion and ideas continue to flow as well as encouraging other directors to change their thinking hats to get as many ideas as possible. With these thinking styles put together, the committee of directors has a much clearer picture of the situation and its possible outcomes and is able to make decisions accordingly.

**Example 2**: This time, you are in a group of designers who are tasked to redesign your company's product package. The flow would then be something like this:

First, everyone puts on the White Thinking Hat to discuss what they know about the package. What does it look like? How do our competitors design their packages? What do the customers say about our package? How well-received is that of our competitors?

Then, everyone proceeds to the Yellow Thinking Hat and identifies the advantages of redesigning the package, its process, and what the product can benefit from the new design. So, you can ask about the benefits of the redesign or what positive impact the new design brings.

From there, the whole team puts on the Black Thinking Hat and looks at the disadvantage of the design change. They discuss the negative impacts on product sales and marketing targets. Here, everyone looks at the risks associated with the design change.

Everyone then proceeds to the Red Thinking Hat, reflecting their emotional reactions toward the current package and the new one. How does everyone feel about the current package? How does it compare to the new one? What do the customers feel about the new design? How does the team feel about changing the current design?

In the Green Hat thinking phase, everyone starts to think of the new design from a creative and innovative perspective. This helps the team think about the new design and how they can improve upon the previous one by looking at its design flaws.

Throughout the entire decision-making process, the moderators wear the Blue Hat to keep the ideas and discussions going and direct them in a way that facilitates the session.

As you can see, the Six Thinking Hats model allows us to view a situation from various standpoints, giving us the chance to further analyze the situation to gain an in-depth understanding. Moreover, this model also provides us with a systematic thinking method by covering the topic from different approaches. This kind of organized thinking can lead you to an ideal solution in the decision-making process.

## The Paul-Elder Critical Thinking Framework

Back in 2002, Paul and Elder introduced a new critical thinking framework to assist students to sharpen their critical thinking skills by identifying thinking parts and evaluating their usage. The goal of this framework aims to improve our reasoning by identifying its different elements by looking at three main elements: reasoning, intellectual standards, and intellectual traits.

### Elements of Reasoning

We use different thinking types to understand an issue. Even in our Six Thinking Hats model, they all have eight common elements. This is similar to the elements of thoughts we have discussed previously. Here, we look at:

- Purpose: Defining a goal or objective such as solving a problem or achieving a target.
- Attempt: What is the previous experience to solve a similar problem?
- Assumption: Before we proceed to solve the problem, we may know little about it. So, we can use assumptions as thebasis of our research. Normally, we start with inductive assumptions and then conduct additional research to validate these assumptions.

- Point of view: We look at our thinking styles here. The Six Thinking Hats model is a good example.
- Data, information, and evidence: This covers all the information related to the issue we are trying to solve.
- Concept and ideas: This covers principles, models, and theories related to the topic.
- Inferences and interpretations: This is how we conclude solutions based on all the previous parts.
- Implications and consequences: Every reason should lead to consequences that result from the implementation of the reasoning process.

**Intellectual Standards**

Reasoning elements need to have a good standard to achieve their purpose and ensure the accuracy of results. There are nine factors you can use to determine whether the parts above are of good quality. They include clarity, accuracy, precision, relevance, depth, breadth, logic, significance, and fairness. To evaluate the parts, you can ask a few questions based on these factors:

- Clarity:
    - Can you explain?
    - Can you give me an example?
    - Can you illustrate what you mean?
- Accuracy:
    - How can we verify that?
    - How can we determine if this is true?
    - How can we test that?
- Precision:
    - Can you be more specific?
    - Can you tell me more about it?
    - Can you be more exact?
- Relevance:
    - How is this related to the problem?
    - How can this help us with the issue?
    - How does that connector the question?

- Depth:
    - What makes this difficult?
    - What are the difficulties we need to deal with?
    - What are the complexities of this problem?
- Breadth:
    - Is there a need to look at this problem from another angle?
    - Do we need to consider another point of view?
    - Should we look at this problem in other ways?
- Logic:
    - Does this make sense together?
    - Is the flow of ideas logical?
    - Does the evidence support the claim?
- Significance:
    - Is this the most important problem to consider?
    - Is this what we need to focus on?
    - Which of these things are the most important?
- Fairness:
    - Is my thinking justifiable in this context?
    - Did I consider what others think?
    - Is my purpose fair given the situation?

**Intellectual Traits**

After applying all of the reasoning elements and verifying those using intellectual standards, you should expect the following to be developed:

**Humility**

You know the limitations and the circumstances that may cause biases and self-receptivity. It depends on whether you recognize that people only claim what they actually know.

**Courage**

Courage here means that you can now address ideas fairly regardless of your personal biases or emotions against their points of view. It helps us develop our ability to evaluate ideas despite our perceptions and presumptions against it.

**Empathy**

Empathy is all about developing the ability to see the world through another person's point of view to understand them. Moreover, it demonstrates how others have arrived at their conclusions so that we may be able to enhance our understanding of the problem at hand.

**Integrity**

This part is related to developing one's ability to combine with the reasoning of others and avoid confusion of our own reasoning. Integrity focuses more on the ability to comprehend others' reasoning of the topic and integrate it to solve the problem effectively.

**Perseverance**

This trait focuses on facing the truth of the situation in spite of all the difficulties or other unpleasant information you have to take in such as difficulties, frustration, and obstacles. This allows you to build more rational reasoning and prepare for difficulties as they happen.

**Confidence in Reason**

When you apply the reasoning elements and encourage people to come up with their own reasons behind their understanding, they build confidence in their reasoning and think in a more rational way.

**Fair-Mindedness**

This trait develops your ability to look objectively at everything without interfering with your emotions, interests, or biases.

With all of these three key components combined, we can understand our thought process better and know how to evaluate our own reasoning systematically. The Paul-Elder critical framework allows you to analyze your own thought patterns and work to improve them.

# The Ultimate Guide to Critical Thinking

Developing and improving critical thinking skills is considered a life study and it is a skill that is worth improving on and pursuing in life. For most educators, critical thinking skills are believed to be one of the most essential skills for life beyond school education. Learning how to think critically is not easy, but it is something that we can improve and learn. If critical thinking was easy, everyone would have the ability to do so. However, it is still the most important skill we need to have in life. We are all aware of the universal concept that there are a lot of definitions, views, and opinions on what critical thinking really is.

We will provide you with tools and resources to be able to reflect independently on the exploration of critical thinking and you can define critical thinking for yourself. You will also be able to develop this skill in yourself, in children, and other people.

We have collected some definitions of critical thinking from other websites that discuss the meaning of critical thinking:

According to the Foundation for Critical Thinking, Critical thinking is the intellectually disciplined process of actively and skillfully conceptualizing, applying, analyzing, synthesizing, and/or evaluating information gathered from, or generated by, observation, experience, reflection, reasoning or communication as a guide to belief and action.

The Stanford Encyclopedia of Philosophy pointed out that critical thinking is a widely accepted educational goal. While the exact definition is highly debatable, they all share a common concept: careful thinking directed to a goal.

Richard W. Paul said critical thinking is thinking about what you are thinking as you are thinking so as to improve your thinking.

Grant Wiggins also said that thoughtful people think about what they learn and the result of what they do. They take all the assumptions and implications of ideas and actions to the table, examine them, and challenge them if needed.

For us, what we define as critical thinking is all about clear, rational, logical, and independent thinking. In order to improve critical thinking, we have to improve the way we think by analyzing, evaluating, and reconstructing. Critical thinking is also about the self-regulated and self-corrective manner in the way we think. Critical thinking also involves communication and problem-solving skills, and we definitely have to avoid any form of bias or what we call egocentric tendencies. We can think critically to apply it in any kind of situation or problem you want to solve.

## Developing Critical Thinking

We have already learned what critical thinking is and why it is important, so now it is time to learn about how we can develop and build critical thinking skills. According to Wabisabi Learning, they have developed a number of useful resources that we can use to develop critical thinking skills. These include:

Critical Thinking Skills Cheat sheet: it consists of questions that you can use to exercise your critical thinking skills whenever you want to discuss new information. These questions can be broadly applied in many situations. These questions are Who-questions.

The following is the ultimate cheat sheet for critical thinking from Wabisabi Learning

WHO
Who benefits from this?
Who have you also heard discuss this?
Who is this harmful to?
Who would be the best person to consult?
Who makes decisions about this?
Who will be the key people in this?
Who is most directly affected?
Who deserves recognition for this?

WHAT
What are the strengths/weaknesses?
What is the best/worst case scenario?
What is another perspective?
What is most/least important?

What is another alternative?

What can we do to make a positive change?

What would be a counter-argument?

What is getting in the way of our actions?

WHERE

Where would we see this in the real world?

Where can we get more information?

Where are there similar concepts/situations?

Where do we go for help with this?

Where is there the most need for this?

Where will this idea take us?

Where in the world would this be a problem?

Where are the areas for improvement?

WHEN

When is this accepted/unaccepted?

When will we know we've succeeded?

When would this benefit our society?

When has this played a part in our history?

When would this cause a problem?

When can we expect this to change?

When is the best time to take action?

When should we ask for help with this?

WHY

Why is this problem/challenge?

Why should people know about this?

Why is it relevant to me/others?

Why has it been this way for so long?

Why is this best/worst scenario?

Why have we allowed this to happen?

Why are people influenced by this?

Why is there a need for this today?

HOW

How is this similar to_____?

How does this benefit us/others?

How does this disrupt things?

How does this harm us/others?

How do we know the truth about this?

How do we see this in the future?

How will we approach this safely?

How can we change this for our good?

## 5 Steps to Asking Good Questions

Critical Thinking Questions

Critical thinking is all about questions. We need to ask questions in order to find out more information related to our problems. Asking questions is a skill that we can practice every day. Asking questions plays a very significant role in developing critical thinking. If we ask good and the right questions, we will receive useful and right answers that we can use to solve the problem.

The foundation of learning, living, and of course, critical thinking is asking good questions. It is believed that much of our success comes from asking good and right questions. Asking good questions can prepare you for the right path to follow in both study and critical thinking. We will show you how you can really do it. It is a simple process from Wabisabi Learning.

Focus:

What do I want to know exactly?

What information am I missing?

Is this more than a simple Yes or NO question?

Am I going for deeper knowledge?

Purpose:

Why am I asking this?

Do I want to gather facts or opinions?

Do I need simple clarification?

Do I want to offer a different perspective?

Intent:

How do I want people to respond?

Do I want the answer that is useful to others?

Do I want to start an argument or open a discussion?

Is the question superficial and not really useful or important?

Am I asking out of frustration or curiosity?

Do I really care about the answer?

Am I willing to show respect/deference to the person I am asking?

Framing:

Am I using easily understandable terms and working?

Is my question neutral or does it contain bias or opinion?

Is it too long or too short?

Does it contain the focus of what I want to know?

Does the question focus on only one thing?

Is it muddled with other inquiries that don't belong?

Am I using easy words to make my questions understandable?

Is my question neutral or does it have any bias or opinion?

Is it too long or too short?

Does it lead to the answer I want?

Does it focus on only one thing?

Did I go off the tangents with my line of questioning?

Follow-up:

Do I have any more questions I should ask? What else did I miss?

Will the person be available to answer my question?

If I still am not satisfied with the answer, what then?

What can I do if I still don't understand?

Other than that, there are games and activities that you can do to engage your critical thinking on multiple levels. We can use the following critical thinking games to develop teamwork skill and collaborative ability.

We have got some stories and scenarios that are based on ethics and morality from Wabisabi Learning that we can use to think critically.

Tom found an expensive phone in the school hallway. There is no way to tell whom it belongs to and it is not near anyone's locker:
Should he
1. Give it to lost and found
2. Ask if it belongs to anyone there
3. Keep it and not say anything

Cade's friend is worried about an upcoming test. If she flunks it, she will fail the entire semester and be unable to graduate with Cade and her other friends. Cade took the test previously, got 100%, and remembers all the answers.
Should she
1. Tell her friend the answers
2. Offer to coach her friend
3. Not get involved at all

Hank overhears two students boasting about how they posted inappropriate pictures of female students online just to get a laugh. He is friends with them, but he knows that this is not the first time they have done something like this.
Should he
1. Mind his own business
2. Report the incident to the school principal
3. Confront the boys and defend the student

You witness a bank robbery and follow the criminal down an alleyway. He stops at an orphanage and gives them all the money.

Would you
1. Report the man to police since he committed a crime
2. Leave him alone because you saw him do a good deed

An old friend of yours tells you that he or she has received death threats online. They also mentioned that the messages have been relentless, which prevents them from focusing. They are too afraid and this has affected their grades. You know of a few people who may be behind this.

Would you
1. Tell your friend just to ignore them
2. Encourage them to report the abuse
3. Risk confronting the ones you suspect

# Chapter 7: Common Critical Thinking Pitfalls and How to Avoid Them

In this chapter, we will discuss some of the most common critical thinking mistakes and manipulations that people use to sway opinions and alter the truth. Before we get into that, let us go back to the basics and understand critical thinking a bit more.

## Three Basic Building Blocks of Critical Thinking

The three basics of critical thinking: Claims, Issues, and Arguments

These are the three basic building blocks of critical thinking; claim, issues and arguments and critical thinking is all about these three elements. We have to be able to identify, separate, and analyze these three elements.

## Claim

In the previous paragraph, we have already mentioned the claim. Claim is one of the three basic elements in critical thinking. Claims are what we say aloud or write down. We use it to convey information and express our beliefs and opinions. This is the primary use of a claim. Claims can also be statements that can be true or false. For example, Alaska is the biggest state in America. It is a true claim. Another example, Alaska is the most populous state in America. This is a false claim as Alaska is not the most populous state in America. There is life living on other planets. This is either true or false as we do not know yet which planet. Again, this is the main role of critical thinking, which is to examine and evaluate the claims being made including their relationships to each other. It is a principal task of critical thinking.

The claim that we are discussing here can be about anything - from small and modest interests or earth-shaking ones. Claims about whether water can help whiten your skin, whether beer can make you fat, whether the president should step down or that war will take place; everything is fair game.

There are many claims that require little or no critical evaluation. They are just obviously true or false that no one has a doubt or needs any critical examination. This can be, for example, whether a shop nearby is still open requires only a phone call and not an investigation. However, there are still a lot of claims that require a close look and examination. It can be a claim about your personal decisions. For example, should you propose marriage to a girl whom you just saw at the corner of the street? It can also be social matters; for example, should we have a capital penalty for rapists? Moreover, if you hold an important position and have to make a decision that will affect other people, it requires you to have a careful examination and evaluation on the claim.

## Issues

This is the most important part of the matter. When we want to turn a claim into a question and when we want to know the truth or falsity of the claim, this is where the issue comes up. Claims turned into issues and supported by arguments are the main point of critical thinking. The issue has a very simple concept as it is described as nothing more than a question. Sometimes, we can use both words interchangeably. What is the question? The question is simply raised in order to know whether or not the given claim is true.

Here are two ways that we can use to state an issue:

1. By asking a question, is John taller than Mark?
2. Whether John is taller than Mark.

When we can answer either one of the two questions, the answer will determine whether the claim "John is taller than Mark" is true.

Another example is Singaporean lawmakers do not like the recent fashion of young people who have dyed their hair red, and they want to make a law that states it is illegal to have red hair. Then, in parliament, the claim "it should be illegal to have red hair" was under consideration or we can say: Whether it should be illegal to have red hair was the issue before the Singaporean lawmakers. It is important to remember that when we think about a claim critically, we turn it into a question and make it an issue.

Sometimes, there is no point for you to consider an argument for or against a claim if you do not have any idea what would be needed toward it being true or false. That means you cannot find any evidence to support your claim in order to say that the claim is true or false.

We really have no idea how to argue or support the claim. For instance, there is no one identical to you who live in a different dimension.

This does not mean that it is worth only discussing the claims that can be proven by scientific or experimental methods. Sometimes, claims are made in contexts which are not really important to know whether the claim is true or not. For example, people tell you a joke. Even though the truth is really necessary, scientific methods are not necessarily needed to prove it. The same way in mathematics, the mathematical theory is not confirmed by experimentation but rather the deduction from other mathematical hypothesis. Some people believe that if the proof is revealed in the Bible, it means it is a true claim. Therefore, you have to have some ideas about what is needed to be used for and against a claim's truth if you are really serious about finding the truth about a claim.

## Arguments

We have already identified what the claim is, and the issue is. Now, let's move to another one which is about argument to weigh the reason for and against the claim with an attempt to determine the truth and falsity of the claim. This is where argument comes into play. Argument is one of the three basic building blocks of critical thinking and it is the most essential ingredient in critical thinking. At the core of an argument, it is a bit difficult to understand, but to put simply, we produce an argument when we want to give a reason for thinking that the claim is true. For example, there is an issue happening with Smith. We will take a look at whether Smith should be excused for being absent from the class. Smith speaks with his teacher. "My mother passed away and I had to skip class in order to attend the funeral." So here, Smith has offered a reason for thinking he should be excused for being absent from the class, so he has made an argument. For now, let's keep it simple, there are a couple more terms that are used in talking about arguments. A claim given as a reason for believing in another claim is a premise. The claim that the premise should give a reason is called a conclusion of the argument. To make it clear, the issue is "whether Smith should be excused for being absent from the class" or another way if you want to change is "Should Smith be excused for being absent from class?"

Premise: Smith's mother passed away and he had to skip class to attend the funeral.
Conclusion: Smith should be excused for being absent from the class.

The role of the conclusion here is to answer the question asked by the issue. The conclusion states a position on the issue.

There are two components to the premise's support of the conclusion. First, the premise can be used to support the conclusion only if the premise is true. In order to see the truth of the premise, we then need to do an independent investigation and we also need more arguments in order to support this claim. Second, the premise that is going to support the conclusion should be relevant to the conclusion. It can sometimes be called Cogent. The two requirements above will indeed show that if the premise, if true, must actually bear on the truth of the conclusion, then it will really increase the likelihood that the conclusion is true.

An argument comprises of two parts. One is the premise or premises, and it will tell us the reason for thinking that the conclusion is true.

**What Arguments Are Not**
In critical thinking, when we use the word "argument," we are not talking about two people having a feud about something. It is important to remember that we do not even need two people. We can use arguments in our own critical thinking all the time.
It is also important to understand that not everything that looks like an argument is an argument. Sometimes, it is nothing more than just a fact.

For instance, there are 5 thieves in a bank robbery, and more people have learned how easy it is to get into a bank where there are lots of people. The local police department reminds all banks in the city to keep a close watch and strengthen their security.

Even though these statements are related to each other by talking about the same topic, none of them acts as a reason for believing the other and, therefore, there is no argument.

Another different example: the number of people who have learned to hack bank accounts has increased in the past year, so you are more likely to be the victim of this scam now than you were a year ago.

So here, the first claim gives support for believing the second claim. We have an argument in the sentence that shows the reason why we are more likely to be the victim of this scam now than you were a year ago.

## Arguments and Explanations

There are a lot of words that often confuse people about arguments such as rhetorical flourishes, asides, tangents, jokes. We need to go through all of these things before arriving at the actual argument. In addition, an argument can also be confused with two common kinds of things, which are explanations and persuasion.

Basically, the role of an argument is to offer support or to prove a conclusion, while an explanation tells us more about what caused something, how something happened, how it works or what it is made out of and so on. For instance, you argued that a dog has a bad smell. This is an argument about a dog, and you want to know why the dog has a bad smell. Then, we need an explanation. Another example, domestic violence has increased over the past few years, an argument, while to know why domestic violence has increased over the past few years is an explanation. Argument and explanation are two completely different things and they always confuse people easily.

## Argument and Persuasions

Some people define an argument as an attempt to convince someone of something. This is not right. The role of an argument is to support and prove a conclusion. When you want to win someone over with your opinion, you will try to persuade them and argue. It is true that you may use argument when you want to persuade someone of something, but not all of those arguments used to persuade and attempt to persuade involve argument. It is the fact that giving arguments is not the most effective way of convincing people.

## Two Kinds of Good Arguments

There are two good arguments, which are good deductive and good inductive arguments.

**Deductive arguments**

It is the first type of good argument, a good deductive argument. If a good deductive argument is valid, it is not possible for the premises to be true and the conclusion false.

Premise: Sam lives in Tokyo.
Conclusion: Therefore, Sam lives in Japan.

This is a valid argument because it is not possible that Sam lives in Tokyo and he does not live in Japan.

Another example,
Premise: Mark is taller than his girlfriend and his girlfriend is taller than her mother.
Conclusion: Therefore, Mark is taller than his girlfriend's mother.

This is also a valid argument because it is not possible for Mark to be taller than his girlfriend and not taller than his girlfriend's mother.

In short, the premises of a good deductive argument, assuming they are true, will surely prove or support the conclusion.

**Inductive Argument**

The premise of a good inductive argument does not prove or demonstrate the conclusion but just supports it. It only raises the probability of being true to the conclusion.

Premise: Alex lives in Belgium.
Conclusion: Therefore, he loves drinking beer.

In this example, Alex lives in Belgium, and it is more probable that he loves drinking beer.

The Language of Arguments

Besides the word "therefore," there are other words that work the same way to show the conclusion. These include
- It follows that...
- This shows that...
- Thus...
- Hence...
- Consequently...
- Accordingly...
- So...
- My conclusion is...

All of these words and phrases have been used everywhere not only as a conclusion indicator, but we always assume that what follows them is a conclusion of an argument.

We also have words that show the premise to be stated:
- Since...
- For...
- Because...
- In view of ...
- This is implied by...
- Given...

Once again, some arguments do not consist of any words indicating a conclusion, and we have to pay attention to whether the statement is going to support or demonstrate something.

## Vagueness

Vagueness, perhaps, is the most common form of unclear thinking or writing. When a word or a group of words is vague, it has an unclear meaning. It is not clear at all for us to understand, interpret, and express. It contains a vague meaning that requires more than just simple reading to understand.

Vagueness plays a very significant role in our legal system. In law, we have to deal with vagueness carefully. Otherwise, it will have many different interpretations in its meaning from various people when we want to apply it in a real situation.

# Ambiguity

A word, phrase, or sentence that is said to be ambiguous contains more than one meaning. For instance, does "John cashed a check" mean that he gave cash to somebody or somebody give cash to him? "Sophie is renting her apartment" can mean she is renting her apartment to someone or she is renting her apartment from someone.

Most of the time, the interpretation that a speaker or writer wants to make for a claim is obvious, but the ambiguity can still happen and its consequences will not just make you smile.

## Semantic Ambiguity

One claim can have several ways of ambiguity, but the most common one is that a claim contains an ambiguous word or phrase that can lead to what we call "Semantic ambiguity."

## Grouping Ambiguity

It is actually a kind of semantic ambiguity that is not clear whether the claim refers to the whole group collectively or each individual member of the group. For example, teachers make more money than doctors.

This example is true if it refers to teachers and doctors collectively because there are more teachers than doctors. However, it is obvious that the example is false if it refers to individual doctors and teachers. It is not different from other ambiguities that can affect the way we think about the claim as it may interfere with our thinking.

## Syntactic Ambiguity

Syntactic ambiguity happens when there are more interpretations on the claim due to its structures, or the construction of the words in the claim that can give the wrong meaning of the claim. Sometimes, we can call it grammatical ambiguity as it involves the grammatical structure of the sentence. For example, the chicken is ready to eat. Now, let's consider this statement. This statement can express two meanings if we do not analyze it correctly. Firstly, it can mean that the chicken is ready for feeding or needs something to eat. Secondly, it can also mean that the chicken is already cooked and ready for us to eat.

## The Claim and its Sources

There are two things that we can use to evaluate credibility. The first thing is the claims themselves, and the second thing is the claims' sources. If we are told that a dog can fly in the air, we will dismiss this claim immediately because such a claim already has no credibility no matter where it is from. It is so obvious that the claim has no credibility and we must not believe it. However, if we are told that ducks mate for life, it is a credible claim, but we need to find the source of the claim to know whether to believe it or not. Moreover, if we can find the information related to this claim in a bird book or research from an expert, we are more likely to believe in the claim.

## Evaluating the Content of the Claim

Some claims express their own true meaning within the claims themselves, and we tend to believe in them regardless of who made them or where they came from. It is so obvious that it is a credible claim. However, when a claim does not stand up to its meaning, it is because the claim is in conflict with either our own observation or background knowledge.

## Personal Observation

Personal observation is one of the most reliable sources of information in the world. Therefore, it is reasonable to feel doubt about any claims that have a direct conflict with what we have observed. For example, you have just come from the home of John, a mutual friend of yours and David's, and you have seen his new black Range Rover vehicle. You meet David and he tells you that John has just bought a new Range Rover vehicle, a red one. In this case, you do not need to have critical thinking skills to reject David's claim because it is so obvious that the claim is in direct conflict with what you just observed when you were in John's home.

### Factors that Influence Our Observation

Our observations can be influenced by several factors and our recollection of them. The factors influencing can be from a physical condition such as bad lighting, lots of noise, the speed of the event, and more. It is also crucial to keep in mind that people are not equally created when it comes to making an observation. Our hope, beliefs, fears, and expectations can also affect our observation. If you tell someone that your house is like a home of rats, they are more likely to believe it if they see the evidence of rats. Moreover, our personal biases and interests are other factors that can affect our perception and judgment. Sometimes, we may not look at the selfishness and greediness of the people we like or love, and if we are inspired by someone, everything that that person does seems to be amazing. Naturally, people who we do not like can hardly do anything that we don't think is selfish and self-centered. If we want to be successful in doing a project, we need to see more evidence for success than is actually presented. In addition, if we want to see a project fail, we tend to exaggerate the flaws that we see in it and imagine that we do not see any problem in the project at all.

**Background Knowledge**

We can have background knowledge by learning from our own observation and from others. The word background implies the information we learned sometime in the past and we cannot specify where or when we learned this information. Most of our background information is well confirmed by a variety of sources and we will dismiss any claims that are in conflict with the store of background information even if we cannot prove it wrong through direct observation. "Mango trees grow in abundance in the North Pole" we will reject this claim immediately even if we are not supposed to confirm or reject the statement by direct observation. When we first encounter such a claim, we have to treat the claim by making a rough assessment of how credible the claim seems to us. We assess the claim by using our background knowledge or information to see the consistency of the claim-like how likely it is to be true with that claim or information. If the claim is consistent with our background knowledge, we will give the claim some degree of credibility. However, if it is in conflict with our background knowledge or information, we will give the claim a low degree of credibility or reject the claim if there is no further evidence to be shown or proved.

# Fallacy

Fallacies are shortcomings that can affect or weaken your argument, and make your argument less effective. The idea of fallacy is to argue that someone holds views that are not really what other people believe. You will be able to be good at evaluating the arguments you read and hear if you can find them on your own and in others' writing. There are two things that you have to keep in mind in fallacy. The first is that fallacious arguments happen very often and are quite convincing, at least to people who are weak in critical thinking. You usually see a lot of fallacious arguments in magazines, newspapers, and other sources. The second one is that, sometimes, it is quite difficult to tell if the argument being made is truly fallacious. You can be told a weak, somewhat weak, somewhat strong and/or very strong argument. An argument that has several parts may contain some strong sections and some weak ones. In this section, we will help you look critically at your own arguments and move them away from the weak to the strong ones.

## Types of Fallacy

For all of the following points, we will explain, and give an example on how you avoid fallacies in your own arguments.

### Hasty Generalization

Hasty generalization involves making the assumption about a group of things or people based on a small or little sample, and usually, the sample is not adequate enough to make that assumption.

Example: "My colleague told me that mathematics class is very difficult and I also had that experience too." All mathematics classes are difficult. By using these two opinions, we cannot make a general assumption that all mathematics classes are difficult. It is just not enough to come up with this conclusion.

In order to avoid this fallacy, you need to look at the kind of sample you are using. Did you come to this conclusion based on your own experience in a few situations? Did you just rely on the views and experiences of a few people? In this case, you need to ask yourself whether further evidence and information is needed to make a conclusion. Exactly. You will have to have more evidence to make a conclusion about mathematics classes in this case.

### Appeal to Authority

When we want other people to believe what we are trying to claim, we often tend to refer to our respected sources or authorities and explain their role or position in the issue we are discussing. If we want to get our readers or listeners to totally agree with us by giving them a famous name or appealing to an authority who is not really an expert in this field, we are trying to make an appeal-to-authority fallacy.

For example, the death penalty should be removed. Many famous and respected people, such as singer Guy Handsome, have expressed their opinion against this law.

In this case, singer Guy Handsome is included as an authority who is believed to be respected in order to make people follow the claim. The point is we should not follow any claims just because it contains someone famous or respected in the claim without thinking about it critically.

There are two ways that you can use to avoid committing appeal to authority. First, we have to make sure that the authority we rely on has to be an expert on the subject we are discussing. Second, not just because "Dr. Authority believes XXX" so we should believe XXX too." What we should do is try to explain the reasoning or evidence that shows how the authority used to arrive at his/her opinion. The authority's reputation is not more important than the source and evidence of his/her opinion.

**Appeal to Pity**

This appeal will take place when an arguer wants you to agree or believe in his/her claim by making you feel sorry for someone.

For example, "I understand that the exam is graded based on my performance, but you should give me good scores. I have been sick for the past several days, and my motorbike is broken, so I didn't have enough time to study."

The conclusion from the arguer is "You should give good scores," but the requirement for getting good scores is based on learning. The arguer wants us to accept that people who have a hard week deserve good scores; which is unacceptable. The information given by the arguer to get us to agree with it is not logically relevant. As a result, the argument is fallacious.

The thing to remember in order to avoid committing appeal to pity is to make sure that you are trying to get your audience to agree with you by making them feel sorry for you or someone.

**Appeal to Ignorance**

For an appeal to ignorance, the arguer basically tries to say that "There is no conclusive evidence on the issue at hand." Therefore, you should believe my claim for this reason.

For example, "For centuries, people have been trying to prove that God does exist, but no one has been able to prove it. Therefore, God does not exist." There is also a different claim about God. "For centuries, people have been trying to prove that God does not exist, but no one has been able to prove it yet. Therefore, God does exist." For these two claims, the arguers are trying to make the conclusion true just because of the lack of explanation and evidence to prove at the present time.

In order to avoid committing appeal to ignorance, you should closely observe the arguments that have no evidence and then come up with a conclusion from the lack of evidence.

**Ad Hominem and tuquoque**

These two types of fallacy focus on the person who makes the claim rather than the quality of the claim itself. The word Ad Hominem means "against the person" and tuquoque means "you too." In these two fallacious arguments, arguers tend to attack the opponents instead of the opponents' evidence or reasoning.

For example, "Andreas Fisher has written several articles trying to argue that online pornography has a negative effect on women. But Andreas Fisher is ugly and bad, so why should we listen to her argument?" The arguers are trying to attack her beauty as being ugly to say no to her argument, instead of trying to prove that her argument is wrong by having good reasoning and evidence to support it. Her beauty has nothing to do with the strength of her argument. Thus, using her beauty as the evidence is fallacious.

In tuquoque, the arguers are trying to show why we should believe this claim if the person who makes the claim also does what they are arguing and so the opponent's argument should not be taken into account.

For instance, there is a family where a father smokes and is always trying to tell his son that smoking is bad. He has given a lot of good reasons why his son should not smoke such as it damages health, costs and so forth. However, the son replies back to his father that "I won't accept what you have just said because you also used to smoke when you were my age." You did it too. The thing here is the father has done something that he is arguing about, so it has no bearing on the premises he is putting in his argument. Therefore, the son's response to his father's argument is fallacious.

The important thing we can do to avoid this type of fallacy is that we should focus on the opponent's reasoning or evidence rather than their personal character. However, if we are about to make an argument about a person's character, it is no longer fallacious to focus on his/her character.

**Ad Populum**

The meaning of this Latin word is "to the people." There are many versions of ad populum but it is usually a type of fallacy in which the arguer takes advantage of the desire that most people have to be liked and uses that desire to get the audience to accept the argument. In other words, the arguer tries to persuade other people to believe in his/her argument because everyone else does.

For example, same-sex marriage is simply immoral. 70% of Americans think so. The opinion of most Americans may influence the American government in determining what law they should have, but it is not certainly relevant to the opponent's argument in determining whether same-sex marriage is moral or immoral. The arguer is trying to make us agree with his/her conclusion by appealing to our desire to fit with the American people.

We have to ensure that we do not try to make other people believe in our conclusion just because many others agree. Always remember that something well-known is always the right one to follow.

**Straw Man**

A man who is made of straw is easier to knock over than a real man. An effective way to strengthen our argument is by anticipating what argument our opponent might make. For the straw man fallacy, the arguers try to make the weak version of the argument that the opponent might make. The arguers sometimes exaggerate or misrepresent an opponent's position. The idea of this argument is to make the opponent's argument look weak so that people will accept our argument. Therefore, the true position of the opponent's argument is not real anymore because it has been exaggerated and misrepresented. It becomes weak and easily rejected and criticized.

For example, there is a conversation between a student and teacher. The student tells the teacher that he thinks some of Donald Trump's position has virtue. The teacher says that he cannot believe that his student supports racist ideas. So here, the teacher assumes that his student will not say something good about Donald Trump because he thinks everyone is against the idea of racism.

The straw man fallacy is so common that it ranks top on our list of the top ten fallacies of all time (see inside front cover). One person will say he wants to eliminate the words "under God" from the Pledge of Allegiance and his opponent will act as if he wants to eliminate the entire pledge. A conservative will oppose tightening emission standards for sulfur dioxide and a liberal will accuse him of wanting to relax the standards. A Democratic congresswoman will say she opposes cutting taxes and her Republican opponent will accuse her of wanting to raise taxes.

**False Dichotomy**

In this type of fallacy, the arguer will try to set up a situation that looks like there are only two possible options that we have to choose from. Then, they will eliminate one of them and make the one left the best choice that you can possibly make. Therefore, we choose the one left or agree with the conclusion. In fact, there are not just two choices, and if we had to think about them, we probably would choose the one left that the arguer recommended.

For example, "you will need to go to a party in the club with me or you will get bored staying at home." This is an example of a false dichotomy. The arguer tries to convince the audience to go to the party as no one wants to stay at home and get bored. The suggestion here is that there are two choices. One is to go to the party and the second one is to stay at home and get bored. The argument neglects to mention the possibility that we might go to do something else besides going to the party or find something else fun to do at home. There are actually, many more possibilities that we can choose to indulge in.

In order to make a good decision and avoid false dichotomy, you need to observe closely the arguments and try to see if there are really only two alternatives available for you to choose. You can ask yourself if there are other options or possibilities besides the two.

**The Genetic Fallacy**

The genetic fallacy occurs when we tend to reject the claim (or urge others to do so) on the basis of its origin, history, and sources rather than its recent meaning or context. They tend to overlook the current position of the claim in the current context and usually, refer to the earlier context as the basis to refute the claim. The claim is accepted as true or false based on the origin of the claim. In genetic fallacy, the source of the claim can be other kinds of entities such as a club, a political party, or an industrial group. For instance, the doctor is overweight, so I don't believe anything he says about improving health. Here, I tend to reject what the doctor said in regards to improving health because he is simply overweight. I think if he cannot even have good health, how can he possibly make me healthy?

## Rhetoric

When you tell a kid that you went water boarding at Guantanamo Bay, they may think that you had one of the best holidays ever. Little do they know that Guantanamo Bay is a prison and water boarding is a form of torture made to simulate drowning? Similar language is used all over the world. "Self-injurious behavior incidents" means attempted suicide. "Detainee" means prisoner. When you hear that a company is "downsizing," you know that someone is getting fired. "Ethnic cleansing" is little more than deportation or genocide.

What we have to say may be important, but the words we choose to use can be just as important. The examples we gave are cases of a certain type of linguistic coercion, an attempt to make you adopt a certain attitude towards a topic. You may be surprised how you can phrase the same exact ideas differently and people will react differently. The words we use have tremendous persuasive power, or what we have called their rhetorical force or emotive meaning. The words we say have the power to express and elicit images, feelings, and emotional associations.

Rhetoric refers to the study of persuasive writing. In this context, it means the use of linguistic techniques to influence beliefs, attitudes, and behaviors. Here is another example:

"Does Julia still owe over $5,000 on her credit card?" and "Does Julia owe a little over $5,000 on her credit card?"

Just by reading this alone, you can tell that there is a major difference between the two questions: the severity. In fact, there is no difference between the two questions, but you feel that the former is a lot more serious. If we allow ourselves to be affected by rhetoric, we fall short as critical thinkers.

Of course, there is nothing wrong with trying to prove a point using rhetoric, using well-chosen, rhetorically effective words and phrases. Good writers do this all the time. However, as a critical thinker, you need to be able to distinguish in an argument its logical force and psychological force through rhetoric. Applying rhetoric to your writing is not wrong. The point here is not to omit arguments or reasoning that is presented in rhetorically charged language, and we are not suggesting you remove all sorts of rhetoric from your own language.

In this section, we will identify common rhetoric to help you identify them as they are presented in an argument, so you can analyze information presented to you objectively.

## Euphemisms and Dysphemisms

Language allows us to say the same thing several times over, and all of them make the listener feel differently. It is the difference between a poet and a politician. Until recently, the term "used car" means a car that is not new. Now, these cars are called "pre-owned," which does not make much sense. The dealers hope that by using different terms, the buyers would feel more inclined to buy their cars because "used" is such a strong word. The term "pre-owned" is a euphemism.

Euphemism is a neutral or positive expression used to hide negative associations. Mainly used by politicians, mass media, and advertisement, euphemisms are key in affecting our attitudes. People may feel less strongly about the assassination of a foreign leader if the act is referred to as "neutralization." People fighting against the government can be labeled as "freedom fighters." A "tax hike" sounds a lot worse than "revenue enhancement program." The United States Department of Defense used to be called the "Department of War."

On the other spectrum, we have dysphemism. Dysphemisms are used to elicit a negative response or attitude from readers or listeners toward something. It can also be used to downplay the positive association it has. So, "freedom fighters" become "terrorists."

Both euphemisms and dysphemisms are often used in deceptive ways. While deceptive, they can be helpful when used properly such as backing a good cause. They allow us to approach a sensitive subject indirectly by preventing a hostile reaction, therefore, grinding a discussion to a halt. They can also be used just to be more polite. For example, "dead" is rough compared to "passed on" So, its uses can also be legitimate.

## Rhetorical Definitions and Rhetorical Explanations

Definitions are intended to clarify meaning and enhance our understanding. When they are loaded with rhetoric, they are intended to change our attitude toward something. When it comes to abortion, how do you define it? Some say it is giving women the chance to live without the burden of raising children, which makes abortion a good thing. Others may define abortion as the murder of an unborn child. So, rhetorical definitions are intended to sway our attitude toward something based on the definition.

Rhetorical explanations are also similar to rhetorical definitions. This time, they are under the guise of explanations. Suppose that your friend lost a fight. He would feel less humiliated if you say that he lost because he was too cautious instead of saying that he lost his nerve. Both are the same because the fact is that he lost the fight, but how it happened can be described differently.

## Stereotypes

A Stereotype is a thought or image of a group of people based on little to no evidence. Thinking that men are insensitive (or stoic if you want to put it that way), women are emotional (or expressive), that gay men are effeminate and lesbians are man-haters are all stereotypes. When you group people under a name or description, especially ones that begin with "the" such as the Communists, the Liberals, the right-wing, the Jews, etc, such labeling often result in stereotyping.

Language that reduces people or things to categories can entice the audience to accept a claim towards those categories without much thought. It can also be used to make quick judgments concerning groups of individuals about whom they know so little.

Stereotypes are mainly used in the political spectrum, which can also involve the ad hominem fallacy. For instance, if you call someone a "left-wing extremist" to defame someone in a political debate, you are using a negative stereotype and an ad hominem (personal attack). So, if we attach a positive stereotype to someone, you create a good impression of that person. If you say that someone is a gentleman, you attach a favorable stereotype, that of a gentleman, to that person.

From where do we get all of our stereotypes? Everywhere, but mainly from the media such as literature, movies, or the news. They are often supported by a variety of prejudices and group interests. Initially, the Native American tribes of the Great Plains were considered to be noble by many white people up until the mid-nineteenth century. From there, white people were more interested in getting these Native Americans to leave, which created a conflict between the two groups. It escalated further and further, and popular literature back then started to describe the Native Americans as subhuman creatures – savages, to put them in a bad light. This stereotype supported the interest of white people. Conflicts generally give birth to some derogatory stereotypes for both sides. Psychologically, it is easier to kill without the pangs of conscience if that person is considered to be less of a human than us. Stereotyping is a lot easier if there are racial differences as well.

When blood pressure gets up and tension is so high, the fact that nothing could have been further from the truth never dawned on anyone. In the heat of the moment is when you need to restrain yourself and think critically of everything. When both sides are armed, and people lose their minds, heads will start rolling unless someone can deescalate the situation.

## Innuendo

When we communicate with other people, we normally have certain expectations and assumptions. For instance, if your teacher says that everybody passed the exam, you would automatically assume that she meant the whole class or those who took the exam. She did not mean that everyone in the world passed the exam. These expectations and assumptions basically give us the context of the situation as it pans out, allowing us to follow along without the other person having to explain everything in meticulous detail. Realistically, no one could be bothered to explain everything all the time, especially in casual conversation. These expectations are important to the success of communication. Innuendo plays on these expectations to sway the opinions of listeners and readers.

For example: "Ladies and gentlemen, I am proof that there is at least one candidate in this race who does not have a drug problem."

Now, this statement is not saying explicitly that any of the opponents of the speaker has drug problems. In fact, the speaker is not denying the fact that other opponents might not have such a problem since the speaker said "at least one candidate." Still, the problem here is that there is no need to say this unless someone among the group has a drug problem. So, the speaker just casts suspicion on all of his opponents. This kind of innuendo aims to get a point across without saying it out loud.

As you can see, the use of innuendo allows us to suggest something bad about something or someone without actually saying it. For example, if someone asks you whether Jane is telling the truth, you may reply, "Yes, this time." This suggests that maybe Jane is not as truthful as the asker may be led to believe. You can say that "Ron is usually helpful," which may suggest that he is sometimes incompetent and unhelpful.

Innuendo does not always have to sound like a neutral statement. You can say something positive about someone and still condemn them at the same time. For example, you can just praise someone a bit when you should have praised them a lot more. In doing so, we hint that the person does not deserve high praise at all, devaluing their efforts. This is another kind of innuendo. For example, after reading a letter of recommendation saying, "Mr. Watson has done some good work for us, I guess," you are not convinced, are you? This letter does not inspire you to hire Mr. Watson immediately. Alternatively, saying "He's been useful so far," or "Surprisingly, he seems very astute," might put him in a worse spot because you assume that he might have done something bad as well to warrant such bland praise. You may notice that the information in these statements is not negative at all. The innuendo lies between the lines, so you need to develop a keen eye to spot it.

# Loaded Questions

Another form of innuendo is the loaded question. If you overheard someone ask, "Have you always loved to gamble?" you would naturally assume that the person being questioned did, in fact, love to gamble. This assumption is independent of whether the person answered yes or no, for it underlies the question itself. Every question rests on assumptions. Even an innocent question like "What time is it?" depends on the assumption that the listener speaks English and has some means of finding out the time, for instance. A loaded question is less innocent, however. It rests on one or more unwarranted or unjustified assumptions. The world's oldest example, "Have you stopped beating your wife?" rests on the assumption that the person asked has in the past beaten his wife. If there is no reason to think that this assumption is true, then the question is loaded.

Another form of innuendo is the loaded question. If someone were to ask you, "Have you always loved to drink?" you would assume that the other person thinks that you love to drink. This assumption is there regardless of the answer because it underlies the question itself. That is not to say that only loaded questions have assumptions. Innocent questions such as "What day is it today?" assume that the one being questioned speaks English and knows how to find out the day. Every question rests on some sort of assumptions. However, a loaded question has a less innocent assumption. It is based on one or more unjustified or unwarranted. The best example we have here is, "Have you stopped beating your wife?" Now, this question rests on the assumption that the person being questioned has beaten his wife in the past.

How do you identify a loaded question? If there is no reason to think that the assumption is true, then the question is most likely a loaded question. How do you answer a loaded question? Jordan Peterson's interview with Cathy Newman is the perfect example here. When she asked him loaded questions, Jordan took a step back and rephrased the questions, taking away their unwarranted assumption. So, someone asks you whether you have stopped beating your wife, just take a step back and say that you have never beaten your wife.

## Weaslers

Weaslers, as the name suggests, protect the person making a claim from criticism by somewhat watering it down, weakening the claim itself, to allow the person to "weasel" his way out if the claim is challenged. They are the linguistic methods of hedging a bet, in a way. Weaslers are commonly used in an advertisement, as you may already be very familiar with. For example, an ad may claim that "Four out of five dentists surveyed recommend sugarless gum for their patients who chew gum." Here, the claim has two weasling expressions.

The first offender is the word "surveyed." The advertisement does not tell us the criteria for choosing the dentists surveyed. Were they chosen randomly or were they dentists who may not be unfavorably disposed toward gum chewing? To make matters worse, there is nothing indicating that the sample of dentists represents the general population of dentists. As far as we know, the sample size could be five, and four of them recommend sugarless gum. Because of this, even if every other dentist on the planet called this ad out, saying that it does not represent the entire population, the author could just say that they only spoke about the surveyed dentists, not all dentists. So, the author could get away with making this claim.

The second offender is "for their patients who chew gum." Did you notice that the ad does not say that any dentists believe that you should not chew gum altogether? The ad only suggests two alternatives: sugar or sugarless gum. Suppose you were to ask the dentists this, "If a patient of yours is adamant about chewing gum, would you prefer that he or she chews gum with sugar in it or sugarless gum?" When you phrase the question this way, of course, any dentists would say that sugarless gum would be a better option. If you were to ask whether people should chew gum without sugar in it, they will say that you might as well not chew gum at all. In this case, the weaslers allow the advertisement author to get away from what is an unqualified recommendation for sugarless gum using facts that have nothing to do to support the recommendation.

Okay, let us make something up. Let's say, a statistic like 99 percent of European doctors don't believe that vaccination is a contributing cause of autism in children, and the remaining 1 percent are convinced. We can then say that "some doctors are convinced that vaccination causes autism in children," and get away with it because we cannot be held accountable for having said something false. Even if our claim is misleading to someone who does know have an in-depth knowledge of the subject, the word "some" allowed us to weasel our way out.

Other words such as "possible," "maybe," and "perhaps," have many uses in the rhetorical context. For one, they can be used to create innuendo to plant a suggestion without explicitly saying it out loud. Doing so allows us to create a claim that is hard to defend. For example, we can say that Tom is a liar without saying it exactly. We can just say that "Tom may be a liar." We can also say that "It is possible that Tom is a liar," which is true for all of us anyway. We lie at some point in our lives. We can also say "Perhaps Tom is a liar," without a problem. These are some examples of how weaslers can be used to create innuendo.

Of course, just because those words are used does not mean that the author is trying to slip in an innuendo to create a way for him to weasel out of. These words can also be used to bring some important qualifications to bear on a claim. It all depends on the context in which the weasel is used. For instance, a detective who is evaluating all the possible angles on a homicide case and just heard Tom's account of the event might say to the police, "Of course, it is possible that Tom is lying." This is not the case of weasling. The detective here is simply exercising due care. So, other words that can be used as weaslers can also be used legitimately. Other qualifying phrases such as "it may well be that" "it is arguable that" and so on can also be used as weaslers. Of course, qualifying phrases are not created equal, and some suggest weasling more than others. For instance, "some would say that" is more commonly used as a weaseling device, although it can be used for an honest purpose in the right context.

So, how can you spot weasling? Well, the only thing you can do is to be careful when qualifying phrases are used. Think whether the speaker or writer is posing a reasonable qualification, using a bit of innuendo, or trying to create a way he could weasel out of? You can only assess what the speaker or writer has said, the context, and the subject itself to determine if the use of a qualifying phrase has an honest intention.

## Downplayers

Downplaying is an attempt to make something or someone look unimportant or insignificant. Downplaying can include stereotypes, rhetorical comparisons, rhetorical explanations, and innuendo. For instance, if you say "Don't mind what Ms. Hank says in class; she's a liberal," you have just downplayed Ms. Hank. This attaches a stereotype to whatever

Ms. Hank has to say. You can also downplay someone or something through careful phrasing using certain words or other devices. Using our previous example, you can say, "Don't mind what Ms. Hank says in class; she's just another liberal." The phrase "just another" denigrates Ms. Hank further. So, downplayers are words or other devices used in order to make someone or something seemingly insignificant.

Other than "just" and "another," two other common downplayers are "mere" and "merely." If your friend Fred tells you that he has a yellow belt in the Tibetan martial art and that his brother has a "mere" green belt, you would normally assume that a yellow belt is ranked higher than a green belt. What we don't know is that a yellow belt is probably ranked lower than a green belt, and he was probably implying that his brother only made little progress although he has been practicing for several years. Here, we can say that Fred's use of the word "mere" gives you the right to make that assumption. Whether or not it is in Fred's intention to not mention that his brother had more experience and is actually ranked higher, Fred was trying to downplay his brother's accomplishment.

The term "so-called" is another standard downplayer. We might say, for example, that the woman who made the diagnosis is a "so-called doctor," which downplays her credentials as a physician. Quotation marks can be used to accomplish the same thing:

You can say that the man who performed the surgery is a "so-called surgeon," which diminishes his credibility as a physician. In written communication, the placement of the quotation marks is also critical because they can be used to emphasize something or downplay something. Take a look at this example:

He got his "degree" from a law school.

The use of quotation marks to downplay something is not to be confused with their other use: to indicate irony. This is an example of irony:

Jack "borrowed" Ben's pen, and Ben hasn't seen it since.

In our second example here, the idea is not to downplay the act of Jack borrowing Ben's pen. The quotation marks are used here to indicate that it was actually not a case of borrowing. The marks around the words "so-called" and "degree" in our previous example are intended to be downplayers, reducing the significance and importance of their subjects. Downplayers are quite obvious, so you should not have too much trouble spotting them.

Other conjunctions such as "still," "but," "however," and "nevertheless" can also be used to downplay claims. These conjunctions are a lot harder to spot because they blend in so well with the claim. Take a look at these examples and try to spot the difference:

Ex 1: Of course, the chemical leak at the plant was a horrible tragedy; however, we should not forget that these pesticide plants are the key in our Green Revolution initiative dedicated to feeding millions of people across the globe.

Ex 2: While it is true that the pesticide plants hold the key to the success of our Green Revolution initiative which has fed millions of people worldwide, it was just such a plant that developed a leak and caused such a horrible tragedy.

The differences between them are not as obvious as those in the cases of "so-called" and "mere," but you can already tell where the sympathies of the authors' are.

Another way to notice the use of downplayers is to observe the context in which the claim is used. Think of the remark, "Mark won only by five votes." The word "only" here may or may not downplay Mark's victory, depending on how thin the five-vote margin is. Let's say that a million people voted and Mark won by five, then the use of "only" is perfectly appropriate. It is not a downplay because Mark literally just won by the skin of his teeth. Alternatively, if the vote was in a committee of nineteen, then five is a substantial margin. Here, Mark would have twelve votes to seven, if everyone votes. The ratio is almost two to one. So, using the word "only" here is obviously a sly device used to make Mark's victory less important than it deserves.

Before you get in trouble, we are not saying that slanters cannot and should not be used altogether. You can use them to give a flair to your writing. What you should avoid is being unconsciously manipulated by these slanters. Finding a well-placed downplayer is a real gem, and you can appreciate how much thought the writer has put into trying to conceal this. Be aware of how these downplayers, subtle or not, can have an effect on you. In doing so, you can protect yourself from being manipulated by a clever speaker or writer.

## Sarcasm

We are all familiar with sarcasm. This kind of rhetorical device is used to ridicule others. It is a powerful rhetorical tool because many of us hate being laughed at as it makes us look incompetent. So, do not be discouraged if someone laughs at your own expense. Just because they laugh does not mean that your argument is any less valid. They haven't even raised their objections to your position.

One might just laugh outright at a claim ("Send aid to Russia? Hah! Good one!"), laugh at another claim because it reminds us of the first ("Take away the Second Amendment Right? Sure, when hell freezes over! Har, har, har!"), tell an unrelated joke to distract you from the discussion, use sarcastic language, or just laugh at the person who is trying to get their point across.

When you are in a debate or watching one, remember that the person who can make the audience laugh the most with the funniest lines has a higher chance of winning the debate. Critical thinkers see differently because they see the difference between arguments and entertainment. That is not to say that there is anything wrong with entertainment in a debate, of course. Being serious all the time makes it boring anyway, even if both sides have good arguments.

## Hyperbole

On the opposite spectrum of downplayers, we have hyperbole. As its name suggests, it is an extravagant overstatement. A claim that exaggerates for effect is considered to be hyperbole, depending on the language used and the points it is trying to get across. For example, it is a hyperbole if someone were to describe a hangnail as a serious injury. It is a hyperbole if someone used the word "fascists" to describe parents who insist that their children have to be home by midnight. Of course, not all colorful or strong language is hyperbole. It depends on the context in which the claim is made. For instance, you can say that "Oscar Peterson is an astoundingly inventive pianist." It is a strong claim, but it is not a hyperbole. It is not that extravagant. But if you were to say "Oscar Peterson is the most inventive musician mankind has ever seen," that is hyperbole. It is beyond emphasis because how can you know that Oscar Peterson is more inventive than Mozart?

Hyperbole can be used in dysphemisms and rhetorical comparisons. When we use the dysphemisms "extremist" or "greedy" to describe the views of a member from an opposing political party, we are using hyperbole. If we say that the general is less informed than an orange, that is hyperbole used in a rhetorical comparison. Similarly, you can use hyperbole in rhetorical explanations and definitions.

Hyperbole is sometimes used in ridicule or sarcasm. If it uses any form of exaggeration, the ridicule is a hyperbole. In our previous example, saying that the general is less informed than an orange is hyperbole used in a rhetorical comparison to ridicule that official.

A claim can be hyperbolic even though the author does not use excessively emotive words or phrases. In our previous examples, neither of them use such language. The word "astoundingly" is the most emotive word in our claim about Peterson, but it is not a hyperbole. Still, a claim can be a hyperbole if we use such language. Saying that "parents who are strict about hanging out with friends are fascists" is a hyperbole, but if we were to replace the word "fascists" with "mean," the claim is still strong and a bit exaggerated, but not hyperbolic. So, when the language becomes excessive and colorful, then the claim is probably hyperbole. It depends on your judgment of the context in which the claim is made.

You can already tell that hyperbole is not subtle in its appearance, but its effect is a lot more subtle. It may even sway your opinions unconsciously. Try as you might to reject it, which is easy to do because it is so blatant, but you may be moved in the direction of the basic claim. For instance, you can reject the claim saying that Oscar Peterson is the most inventive musician, but you may now think that he is a very talented musician anyway. If not, why would someone make such an exaggerated claim about him? Suppose someone says that Taylor Swift is the best singer of all time, and you reject that claim, you at least think that Taylor Swift is a talented singer. This is where you need to be cautious because any claim is just as worthless without reason to support it. Just because the claim is wild does not mean that you should accept it more than ordinary, unsupported claims.

## Proof Surrogates

A proof surrogate is an expression used to suggest that there is evidence or authority for a claim without really citing or presenting them. In some cases, we cannot prove the claim we are trying to assert, but we can at least hint that there is proof or evidence available without actually committing ourselves to them. Phrases such as "many studies" or "informed sources say" are some of the most common ways to make a claim suddenly more authoritative. The thing is, no sources are cited. Who are the sources? How do we know if they are legitimate? How does the person making the claim know that they are informed? "It's obvious that" is also regularly used and it sometimes precedes a claim that is not obvious at all. But when we are told that something is obvious, we may hold back our objections because we think that it is obvious to everyone else but you and because we do not want to appear denser than the next guy. The audience may also have the same thought. In advertisements, "studies show" is often used. Again, this alone does not tell us anything about how many studies were conducted, how good they are, who did them, as well as any other important information.

Remember, proof surrogates are only surrogates. They are not meant to be considered as real proof or evidence. The proof or evidence might exist, but the claim is still unsupported until they are presented. At best, proof surrogates suggest sloppy research. At worst, they suggest propaganda.

## Rhetorical Analogies and Misleading Comparisons

Misleading comparisons are also commonly used, mainly by politicians to promote their agenda. For example, Robert Kittle, who was an editorial page editor for the San Diego Union-Tribune, said that the Social Security system is a Ponzi scheme. If you do not know, a Ponzi scheme is a pyramid scheme intended to get as much money out of its members as possible. What Robert did there was known as a rhetorical analogy. The rhetorical analogy is defined as the comparison of two things to make one of them seem better or worse than it is. Of course, analogies are often used to help you explain something, not necessarily to manipulate.

For instance, if you are trying to explain rugby to a friend of yours who knows nothing about it, you may compare it to football. In our example here, Kittle's comparison is not intended to explain to the reader, but rather to persuade and sway their opinions. Ponzi scheme is such a strong and negative term, and calling something a Ponzi scheme puts it in a bad spot.

People often replace arguments with rhetorical analogies. It is not hard to see why, really. You need facts to prove something is true. In our example, you need to do extensive research to prove that Social Security is financially unsustainable. If anything, it is more convenient to just call it a Ponzi scheme altogether because it may be just as effective anyway. This kind of persuasion works really well as you can persuade the listener without the need to show actual proof. You can also make rhetorical analogies using metaphors and similes, and they still make the audience feel a certain way.

Comparisons also fall under rhetorical analogies. For example, you can say that you have a higher chance of dying in a car crash than in a plane crash. This is a creative way of getting your point across, but just because that is true does not mean that it is a reason for accepting that point.

If we are not careful, we can fall victim to some comparisons. A great example is the vagueness present in advertisements. Their slogans say something like "New and improved formula," or "Now 50 percent larger," or "Quietest by far." With a little scrutiny, you can already tell that these claims are worth little. We have talked about vagueness before. How is it new and improved? 50 percent larger compared to what? Quietest by what standard? Unless the changes are spelled out explicitly, telling you exactly what has been improved, these claims are worth very little.

While we are on the topic of comparison, you may be familiar with discounts at the mall and other sales events. "50% off!" the banners read, "Buy one get one!" Oftentimes, people will flock to buy whatever is on sale, even though they may not have much use for whatever they are buying. But why do people buy things they do not have a use for? You see, we learn how to exploit opportunities or scarcity. We believe that the discount is going to be a once in a lifetime opportunity, so we take it. Being opportunistic is good, but the problem is that we do not think much of the result. Companies learn to exploit this weakness and put up discounts all the time. Their profit margin per product may go down, but the sales will go so high that it compensates for the loss. That is, of course, if they did not mark up the price before the "discount" event. If you sell lollipops for $0.25 a pop, people may not buy them. If you put up a discount sign saying that you are selling four lollipops for $1, you may sell more than you think. What do we learn here? Similar to the example we gave above, it is worth to stop and think carefully about the opportunities you are presented with. Sure, that pair of shoes is 50% cheaper, but it's not worth buying it if you won't use them any time soon anyway.

When faced with comparisons, it is worth asking yourself these five questions. They include references to omissions and distortions, which are some of the most subtle forms of rhetorical devices.

1. Is important information missing? Of course, learning that the unemployment rate went down to virtually zero is a good thing, but the result may be because most of the workforce has just given up on looking for a job. If someone tells you that 75 percent of heroin addicts once smoked marijuana, that does not mean much either without more information. Over 75 percent of heroin addicts have listened to the Beatles at least once, too. That does not tell us anything. A U.S. Congressional Representative, Wally Herger, told his constituents that Social Security is in dire straits, saying once that there were 42 workers to support a single retiree, the number has now gone down to 3. From the get-go, what he claimed seemed ominous. What Representative Herger failed to mention is that the 42-to-1 ratio was only present at the start of Social Security, before many people retired. He also failed to mention that the 3-to-1 ratio has been constant for the last two decades or so, during which Social Security has accumulated a surplus.

2. Is the same standard of comparison used? Are the same practices of reporting and recording used? The fluctuation of the unemployment rate does not tell much if the government changes the way it calculates unemployment, which actually happens sometimes. It is like saying that an athlete managed to jump as far as 200 meters when a meter to you is one centimeter to another. Comparisons cannot be used unless they are measured by the same standard. Back in 1993, the number of people in the U.S. who were HIV positive suddenly skyrocketed. Was there an outbreak? Had a new form of the AIDS virus appeared? No, and no. The federal government just expanded the definition of AIDS to include many other indicator conditions. Suddenly, 50,000 more people were considered to be HIV positive overnight.

3. Are the items comparable? It is obviously difficult to compare who is the better bodybuilder if one of them used steroids and the other did not, or if one had a coach or better equipment. It is hard to draw a conclusion from the fact that this May's retail business activity is much lower compared to last May's if a tornado suddenly hit the local area, causing heavy rain and flooding for the whole month. It is hard to draw a conclusion from the fact that there are more male deaths in traffic accidents compared to female when men often drive farther and longer hours than women. Comparing share values of two mutual funds in the last decade will not tell you any new information if the comparison itself does not consider the difference in fees. So, the comparison should only be done when the two things share values.

4. Is the comparison expressed as an average? The average rainfall in Seattle is about the same as that in Kansas City. But you'll spend more time in the rain in Seattle because it rains there twice as often as it does in Kansas City.

5. Is the comparison expressed as an average? If a company reports that the average salaries of most of its employees have doubled over the last decade, you may assume that it is a great place to work. That is not always the case though. The increase may be caused by the conversion of half-time to full-time staff and firing the rest. Be wary of comparisons that involve averages because they often omit important details, just because they involve averages. The average rainfall in Seattle is roughly the same as that of Kansas City, but you will spend more time in the rain living in Seattle because it rains twice as often, compared to Kansas City. Averages are just measures of central tendency, and there are different kinds of measures or averages. For example, take the average cost of a new house in your area. Let us assume that it is $100,000. If that is the mean, then it is the total of the sales prices divided by the number of houses sold, which may be different from the median. The median is an average that is the halfway figure (half the houses cost more and half cost less). The mode is the most common sales price, which can be again, different. If you are offered an average of anything, be very cautious.

## Persuasion Using Visual Images

In this age, where people can edit a picture of Justin Bieber into a potato, it is much easier to take photographic evidence at face value. Back then, you could not just edit digital photos. Still, there were all kinds of things that could be done to manipulate an image. Even without the tools to edit photos, people still managed to change a viewer's perception of what was going on in the photo. In some cases, you do not even need to edit the photos and videos to create a mistaken impression in the viewer.

Back in 2005, Terri Schiavo, a Florida woman, became the center of a controversy regarding whether she was in a Persistent Vegetative State (PVS) and could be expected to regain consciousness, let alone recover. Her family members took a video of her, which showed that she appeared to be responding to the presence of her mother. A heart surgeon and majority leader of the U.S. Senate, Bill First, also saw the videotape and claimed that Ms. Schiavo seemed to be responding to visual stimuli. On the other hand, other doctors including her own also said that these facial expressions were often displayed by those in PVS, and were not necessarily a conscious response. After her death, an autopsy was conducted showing that Ms. Schiavo's brain had shrunk to half its original size. What was left was a severely damaged brain. Other than that, her visual cortex was damaged as well, which meant that she had been blind for quite some time before her eventual death. The possibility of having anything like consciousness near the end of her life was a medical impossibility.

This is how a simple videotape can be ambiguous. It is open to more than one interpretation, even if it was a raw, unedited video clip. Many viewers can have a mistaken impression which leads them to make false claims. Of course, photos, videos, and other imagery cannot be true or false per se, but claims based on them can be.

Some people perform image manipulations of various sorts to try to create mistaken impressions. How can you identify them? These images can be the result of:

- Deliberately manipulating an image (e.g., adding, deleting, combining)
- Using unaltered images but with misleading captions
- Deliberately selected camera angles that distort information

- Lack of authority (i.e., author name, credentials); inconsistency when compared to official images
- Imagery taken from movies: out of context, they are given false descriptions
- Imagery taken of models purported to be the real thing
- Imagery that is genuine and unadulterated but "staged"
- 100% digital fabrications

It is unrealistic to expect people to be able to identify edited photos and videos wherever they appear, especially with the current technology. No one can do it, to be honest. Some images are so carefully edited that no one but the creator himself knows that they are fake.

So, what can a critical thinker do here? You do what every other critical thinker does: be careful. While there are plenty of people out there trying to inform and educate you, know that there are many more whose objective is to fool you. Take everything with a grain of salt and do not take everything at face value.

# Chapter 8: How Critical Thinking Affects Your Life

Critical thinking is a general thinking skill. In whatever we want and choose to do, the ability to think clearly and rationally is important. Critical thinking is obviously necessary when you have a career in finance, research, education, management, or in the legal field. Still, that does not mean critical thinking skills are restricted to any subject area. Being able to think clearly and solve problems systematically is an important asset to have, no matter which career you are pursuing.

Critical thinking is very important in the new knowledge economy. Information technology is also important in the global knowledge economy nowadays as it is driven by these two factors. Plus, we need to be prepared to deal with constant and rapid changes promptly and effectively. As the fluctuation of the worldwide economy increases, so does the demand for flexible intellectual skills such as the ability to analyze information and utilize diverse sources of knowledge to solve problems. Critical thinking skills help promote these intellectual skills and are essential in the ever-changing workplace.

Critical thinking helps improve language and presentation skills. The ability to think clearly and systematically can help improve the way we present our ideas. Critical thinking also improves our comprehension abilities in learning how to analyze the logical structure of texts.

Creativity also comes from critical thinking. One may need to use ideas and information differently in order to generate creative solutions. Critical thinking can also be utilized to evaluate new ideas, determine whether or not they are useful and relevant, and select the best one or change them if needed.

Good critical thinking is the foundation of democracy and science. Objective use of information and reasoning in experiments is fundamental. In order to run a liberal democracy properly, all citizens need to be able to think critically about social issues that lead to proper governance and to overcome biases and prejudice in society.

We do not want people to just focus on learning and do their work well only in the classroom as the fundamental objective of education is to create a desire to learn more beyond the academic school year. Critical thinking is a lifelong learning process and critical thinkers are also lifelong learners.

We need to start from the basics if we want to discover how critical thinking is related to lifelong learning. Lifelong learning is a self-motivated desire in learning that persists throughout our entire lifetime. However, what makes these people want to continue learning for their entire lifetime? It must be not just about desiring to become a success and for survival. To keep learning, we need to maintain our interest in learning by making sure that the process of learning itself is relevant, focused, and practical. For instance, which of the following have you done recently or in the past?

- Read a book and learned something new
- Watched a YouTube tutorial video on how to fix something
- Participated in any kind of class, course, or training
- Searched on how to do school assignments online
- Learned something from other people including a tutor or a mentor

All of these actions have something in common. These are the activities that a critical thinker might take to fix a problem or answer the question. To people who think critically, all of the information and knowledge from every side is essential and needed. Both critical thinking and lifelong learning share inherent qualities that are the ability to see potential in any approach to learning. Learning for a lifetime shows itself in a number of different ways. The above examples are some of them. We can also learn from other people through socializing, gaining experience in any activities, or simply making observations or mistakes. So, we can develop critical thinking by practicing it whenever we can.

# Chapter 9: Conclusion

That's about it. With all of the knowledge acquired in this book, you are well on your way to improving your critical thinking skills and identifying fallacy and rhetoric in other peoples' arguments.

The key here is to think systematically and go slow if you must. It is always better to think slowly than to decide incorrectly. Having good critical thinking skills puts you way above others in professional and personal fields as you can decide and act in a way that best benefits everyone. One cannot stress enough how important it is to develop your critical thinking skills, especially in this day and age where manipulation and misinformation run rampant.

Thankfully, you are no longer a victim of this falsehood. Your life will be significantly improved thanks to your new way of thinking. Give yourself a pat on the back for reading this far, and good luck on your journey.

# Stoicism

*The Practical Guide to the Stoic Philosophy and Art of Happiness in Modern Life to Help You Develop Your Self-Discipline, Critical Thinking, and Mental Toughness and Live a Better Life*

# Table of Contents

Chapter 1: Introduction .................................................................................. 101

    It Was Built for Hard Times ................................................................. 101

    Stoicism Is Made for Globalization ..................................................... 102

    You're Already Part-Stoic ..................................................................... 103

    Unofficial Philosophy of the Military ................................................. 103

    Philosophy for Leadership .................................................................. 103

Chapter 2: What is Stoicism? ........................................................................ 105

    The Stoics ............................................................................................. 106

    The Main Principles of Stoicism ......................................................... 107

Chapter 3: The History of Stoicism .............................................................. 112

    Early Stoa (300 – 100 BC) – Zeno, Cleanthes, and Chrysippus ........ 112

    Middle Stoa (100 BC – 0) – Panaetius, Posidonius, Cicero, and Cato ........ 113

    Late Stoa (0 – 200 AD) – Seneca, Epictetus, and Aurelius ............... 113

    In Summary .......................................................................................... 114

Chapter 4: Stoicism and Happiness ............................................................. 115

    A View From Above ............................................................................. 115

    Contemplate the Ideal Man ................................................................. 116

    Cultivating Philanthropy ..................................................................... 117

    Self Retreat ........................................................................................... 118

    The Stripping Method ......................................................................... 119

    Negative Visualization ......................................................................... 120

    Physical Self-Control Training ............................................................ 121

    Don't Outsource Your Happiness ....................................................... 122

    Forego Ego and Vanity ........................................................................ 126

    Stand Your Ground ............................................................................. 131

## Chapter 5: On Mindfulness Practices .................................................................... 132
### Stoic Mindfulness .................................................................................................. 132
### Meditation ............................................................................................................. 133
### How to Develop Awareness of Emotions and Thoughts ................................... 138

## Chapter 6: On Consolidation of Thoughts ............................................................ 144
### Philosophical Journal ............................................................................................ 144
### Early Morning Reflection ..................................................................................... 145
### Bedtime Reflection ................................................................................................ 146
### How Journaling Leads to a Better Life ................................................................ 146

## Chapter 7: Overcoming Negative Emotions ......................................................... 154
### Stay Focused ........................................................................................................... 154
### Develop an Internal Locus of Control ................................................................. 154
### Guard Your Time ................................................................................................... 155
### On Trusting the Process ....................................................................................... 160
### On Dealing with Anger ......................................................................................... 162

## Chapter 8: On the Art of Mental Toughness ........................................................ 167
### Deconstruct Things ............................................................................................... 167
### Reframe Negative Events ..................................................................................... 168
### Acknowledge Your Challenges ............................................................................ 169
### Find Your Purpose ................................................................................................ 170
### Recharge and Recover .......................................................................................... 171
### Flex the Muscle ...................................................................................................... 171
### Stay Resilient ......................................................................................................... 172

## Chapter 9: Other Practical Tips and Practices ..................................................... 173
### Add a Reserve Clause – If Nothing Prevents You ............................................... 173
### Love Your Fate ....................................................................................................... 173
### Forgive the Wrongs of Others .............................................................................. 174

Buy Tranquility ..................................................................................................... 175
16 Lessons for Living ............................................................................................. 175
Chapter 10: Conclusion ......................................................................................... 178

# Chapter 1: Introduction

Stoicism is intended to teach us all of how unpredictable the real world can be, and how brief our life is. It teaches us how to maintain mental resilience during hardship and how to be in control of your own emotions. Finally, it addresses the dissatisfaction that lies in our impulsive dependency on reflexive senses rather than logic.

Stoicism does not discuss complicated theories of what the world should be. It merely acknowledges that the world is random and flawed, and advises us to accept it as it is. It focuses on helping us overcome our destructive emotions as a reaction to what the world throws at us, and compels us to act on what can be acted on. Stoicism is practical, built for action, not an endless debate of what should be. It is about sticking your nose into the grindstone and getting things done. But how relevant is Stoicism in modern day society?

Well, let us take a look at Clinton's line on Obama. He struck a familiar chord because he reminded us of another politician known for his coolness. That person is Cato the Younger.

Cato was a practitioner of Stoicism, which was an ancient Greek religion that he brought with him to Rome. It's not that Obama was a Stoic, but we can see the public's response to his self-control. It shows how poorly Stoic qualities can go over in our time. Stoicism was built on emotional control, which seems alien in the age where everyone is sharing everything.

It is a shame, actually. We can learn so much from it, especially when every little thing screams for our attention and tries to control how we should think and feel. Moreover, the Stoic legacy has shaped our world more than you think. There are five main reasons why Stoicism matters nowadays more than ever:

## It Was Built for Hard Times

Hard times create strong people. Strong people create good times. Good times create weak people. Weak people create hard times. The cycle goes on.

Stoicism came around as the world was falling apart. Birthed in Athens a few decades after Alexander the Great's conquests and premature death, Stoicism took off mainly because it gave the people security and pace during the time of war and crisis. Stoicism did not promise material security or peace in the afterlife. However, it did promise unshakable happiness in this life.

Stoicism reminds us that we cannot secure our happiness if we base it on changeable, destructible things. Our careers can grow and wilt, the number on our bank account can rise and fall. Even our loved ones can be taken from us one way or another. So, it is clear that you cannot build a foundation of happiness on external things. There is one thing that the world cannot change. That is our inner selves, our choice to behave in a specific way, to be reasonable, and to be virtuous.

The world can take everything from us. Come what may. Stoicism reminds us that we have a fortress on the inside. Epictetus was born a slave and crippled at a very young age. He wrote, "here is the good? In the will... If anyone is unhappy, let him remember that he is unhappy by reason of himself alone."

It's a natural instinct to cry out in pain, but the Stoics suggest that we stay indifferent to everything that happens outside, and remain equally happy both in time of abundance and scarcity. That is not to say that Stoicism is easy to adopt into your life, but it at least offers us freedom from passion, which is the freedom from the emotions that have controlled our words and actions for a very long time. A real Stoic does feel emotions, but he or she knows how to master their emotions. Stoicism recognizes that emotions such as grief, fear, or greed only enter our mind when we permit them.

A teaching like this seems to be designed for a world on edge, whether it's the chaotic world of ancient Greece or in a modern financial crisis. Then again, Epictetus said that as long as we place our happiness on perishable things, our worlds will always be on edge.

## Stoicism Is Made for Globalization

The world in which Stoicism was born is from a parochial and xenophobic world in which people cling to an age-old division of nationality, religion, and status. Openly embracing those divisions may not be an easy task, but Stoicism encourages us to do so. It was one of the first Western philosophies to preach universal brotherhood. Epictetus said that everyone has ownership of the world we live in. We are all members of the great city of gods and men. Marcus Aurelius, the Roman emperor, as history's well-known Stoic, reminded himself that he loves the world as much as he loves his own people.

If the key to our happiness is in our own will, then even the greatest social dividers seem insignificant. Seneca lived a life of slavery, but he urged others to "remember that those who call you a slave came from the same stock, are smiled upon by the same skies, and on equal terms with yourself breathe, live, and die."

This embrace of world-city, where everyone is of one nation and race, made Stoicism the ideal philosophy for the Roman Empire. This brought together people from different races and religions. Therefore, Stoicism is relevant in a globalized world.

## You're Already Part-Stoic

This has been taught in many religions that humans are under the same creator, God himself. He tells us to moderate and master our impulses rather than giving into them. Of course, we are humans, so we will probably fail this mission. This may sound familiar in your religion because the idea behind this religious philosophy is Stoicism.

Christianity is a deeply Stoic religion. After all, Stoicism dominated Roman culture for centuries. From there, Christianity went mainstream in the same culture. Moreover, many early leaders of the Christian church were former Stoics. So, we know that Christianity borrowed much of its thought and terminology from Stoicism.

Unfortunately, as time went on, church leaders, who wanted to emphasize the uniqueness of their faith, started to downplay the Stoic connection. But we do know that Stoicism was at the foundation of the Christian religion.

## Unofficial Philosophy of the Military

Back in 1965, James Stockdale's a-4E Skyhawk was shot down over Vietnam and he was held as a prisoner of war for seven years without receiving any prisoner rights. We will discuss his life in more details in a later chapter, but he drew strength and determination from Stoicism and survived imprisonment. It helped him confront the grim reality of the situation without giving in to despair and depression. This is what a soldier, student, and office workers alike need to keep in mind their entire life.

## Philosophy for Leadership

Stoicism reminds us not to control things outside our control. Instead, we should strive to control ourselves first. We should not try to exert influence over the world that is always changing as we will be subject to disappointment and failure. Ever since Marcus Aurelius, world leaders have discovered that a Stoic attitude still gets them respect in the face of failure and prevents them from being arrogant in the face of success.

Stoicism gives us courage in the face of uncertainty. Leaders, especially, are subject to risk and change, so it is not surprising to see that many leaders find the philosophy of Stoicism appealing for their mental health. You can see this in Barack Obama's many public appearances and interviews. He displayed a Stoic demeanor.

In short, Stoicism does not guarantee success, but it does guarantee happiness no matter what situation you are in. It guides you on a path of virtue and gives you a realistic view of leading your life.

This is what this book intends to do: introduce you to the ideas of Stoicism and give you practical exercises you can incorporate into your life. Without further ado, let us get into this.

# Chapter 2: What is Stoicism?

Stoicism is basically designed to help individuals lead their best possible lives. It is a philosophy of life that aims to minimize negative emotions and maximize positive ones. Not only that, but it also paves the way for individuals to hone their virtues of character.

Stoicism gives us a framework so we can find order within the chaos of life. This is applicable at any stage of your life, and in many situations. It gives us a sense of purpose by reminding us of what is really important and giving us practical strategies to get more of what is valuable.

Stoicism was created with the intention to be useful, actionable, and understandable. Practicing it is a lot easier than you think, as it does not require any learning nor does it involve meditation for extended periods of time. Here, we focus on methods that are more immediate, useful, and practical so you can achieve tranquility and improve your strength of character.

Stoicism is a school of philosophy with its source tracing back to ancient Greece and Rome in the early 3rd century.

Here, we would like to point out the differences in peoples' thought processes back then. You see, the Stoics provided amazing and compelling answers to questions about our troubles, fear, stress, and anxiety. Ask a friend what does he or she want out of life? Many people cannot answer such an open-ended question, but the Stoics can, and they may offer an operating system that deals with the trials of the human condition.

Whatever it is that people want, it all boils down to happiness and peace of mind that comes not from wealth or titles, but rather by being a virtuous person.

For example, an individual can hone their virtues of character by giving more value on actions instead of words. Basically, positive behavior creates a more positive life experience. The opposite is also true.

In short, stoicism was an ancient school of philosophy that guided us to a more virtuous life, maximizing happiness and reducing negative emotions. Its values have been tried and tested throughout human history by famous individuals such as George Washington, Arianna Huffington, Tim Ferriss, Thomas Jefferson, and many more.

While its guiding principles were established long ago, the stoic's strategies are even more important today than they were in ancient times. Our lives are more chaotic than they were a few centuries ago. So, stoicism is forever relevant to us.

## The Stoics

Stoicism was not established by the hands of Zeno alone. There are many thinkers that helped form the Stoic philosophy. They are:

### Zeno of Citium

The stoic philosophy was founded by Zeno of Citium. He turned his misfortune in the form of a shipwreck that left him stranded in Athens into an opportunity by capitalizing on all the philosophical resources in the city. He attended all lectures from other schools of philosophy such as Cynicism and Epicureanism and then created his own philosophy. The word Stoicism came from the word "stōïkos," which refers to the Stoa Poikile (a renounced painted porch in Athens) from which Zeno preached his theory.

### Marcus Aurelius

Marcus Aurelius, being one of the most influential individuals in our history, was the head of the Roman Empire for two decades. He ruled the empire when it was one of the largest and most influential civilizations in the world. While Aurelius had limitless power, he could do whatever he pleased on a whim with impunity. However, he practiced and lived the Stoic philosophy instead.

As you have already guessed, living a stoic life was not easy. He documented his struggles to lead a restrained, wise, and virtuous life. It was only much later that his personal writings were discovered, collected, and then published under a book titled "Meditations." This is now one of the masterpieces and go-to documents if you wish to know more about stoicism. Aurelius wrote about his own thoughts and practical approaches toward stoicism, strategies you can incorporate into your life to help you cope with stressful situations.

### Lucius Annaeus Seneca

Lucius Annaeus Seneca had a remarkable charisma and a solver's tongue thanks to his occupation as a statesman, a dramatist, and a writer. He had a colorful, straightforward, and entertaining way of describing Stoicism. Thanks to his simplistic approach to teaching stoicism, we recommend that you check out his works if you are new. Moreover, Seneca's thoughts are more relatable for modern audiences because his thoughts are more relevant to us, covering topics such as friendship, mortality, altruism, and the proper use of time.

## Epictetus

Epictetus was once a slave, but his life eventually improved to the point that he became one of the most analytical thinkers of Stoicism. You can find practical strategies to implement stoicism into your life in his handbook titled "The Enchiridion." He had a knack for explaining how stoicism can improve a person's life dramatically and made a compelling case for why everyone should consider making stoicism their primary operating system. Many of his teachings are, though recognizable, tragically uncredited.

## The Main Principles of Stoicism

Initially, Stoicism focused mainly on logic and physics. As time went on, it shifted to more psychological concerns such as wellbeing and tranquility. While the Stoics can never convene to affirm all of their tenants precisely, they all agree on certain principles that form the core of stoicism.

Most importantly, these principles are not just something that you can think about momentarily and then forget about. They should be practiced every day of your life.

## Walk the Talk

"Waste no more time arguing what a good man should be. Be one." – Marcus Aurelius

What does this tell us? We as Stoics should not concern ourselves with worthless and purely theoretical contemplation. Focus on real-world pragmatism instead of pondering just for the sake of it.

Expanding on the idea of pragmatism, in the real world, you need to find answers and act on them. Being a true Stoic is not just about being an armchair philosopher who just rambles on and on about theories. You need to walk the talk, so to speak. Be the person who says what should be done and gets things done.

Moreover, you may notice that the Stoics also have a concern of leading a righteous life. Of course, we have already established that this principle includes taking action and not wasting time pondering what should be. Stoics believe that a good life is one of moral action. So, if you want to live well, be a morally just person.

## Control Only What You Can

"The chief task in life is simply this: to identify and separate matters so that I can say clearly to myself which are externals not under my control, and which have to do with the choices I actually control. Where then do I look for good and evil? Not to uncontrollable externals, but within myself to the choices that are my own..." – Epictetus

In the previous section, we discussed only needing to worry about what we can actually control. If we wish to worry, there are so many things to worry about. Global tension over North Korea, the South China Sea, and global warming are three of the major things out there. The Stoics understand that everyone has no control over everything, even the big guys out there. You cannot control most of what happens in life. If anything, worrying about things outside your realm of control is unproductive, and may irritate you. This prevents you from reaching mental tranquility, which is one of the most important things in a Stoic's life.

In the face of all of these troublesome events, we should all be able to differentiate between what is within our control, what we should worry about, and the things that are not. If you cannot control something, no one will think less of you if you ignore it. After all, there is no point in wasting energy over uncontrollable events. So, whereas others worry and fuss about things they cannot change, the Stoics focus their energy on finding creative solutions instead of on the problems themselves.

## Be Grateful

"No person has the power to have everything they want, but it is in their power not to want what they don't have, and to cheerfully put to good use what they have." – Seneca

Epictetus lived a life of slavery without personal possessions. Even his own body was not his. He hit rock bottom, yet he pursued the Stoic life anyways. Of course, while it focuses more on peace of mind, that does not mean you must forego all material possessions. In fact, the Stoics believe that these possessions serve to increase your happiness and improve your ability to lead a virtuous life. However, be very careful about the hype and power of consumerism that would invade your tranquility of mind and decision-making. Many of us are upset at the things we cannot have. Maybe your neighbor has a more beautiful, expensive car.

Perhaps your boss has a kinder and more beautiful spouse. You may overlook the fact that you are in better health or have fewer problems to worry about.

Another example of poverty is Seneca. He would fast and wear unfashionable clothing to remind himself that people do not need material possessions to live a good life. They are good to have, but not necessary for your peace of mind. In all, almost every one of us has enough to get by and be happy. Still, we are upset about our lives because we keep maintaining our insatiable desire for more.

There is a difference between want and need. Need refers to material things we require to survive, including food, shelter, clothing, etc. These physiological needs are located at the bottom of Maslow's needs hierarchy, meaning that these things are a must-have for survival. You do not need much else from other levels to achieve happiness. On the other hand, want is something we feel that we need, but is actually not necessary for us. If we can live or work without it, then it is probably something you want, not need.

So, what do we learn from this? Stoics try not to suffer over what they do not have. Instead, they focus on being grateful for what they currently have.

## Be Positive

"I judge you unfortunate because you have never lived through misfortune. You have passed through life without an opponent – no one can ever know what you are capable of, not even you." – Seneca

The Stoics have a different view of misfortune. We see it as a tragic incident or a coincidence that does not favor us. They expect mishaps to happen, as they often will, but they use them to hone their virtues instead of mourning about it. Of course, that does not mean that they are happy when they are struck with misfortune. They just try not to lament about it as it changes nothing. Instead, they strive to develop their own character through hardships whenever possible.

For instance, suppose that you got into a road accident and broke both your legs. You need to be hospitalized and bed-ridden for months until they heal. Any normal human being would adopt the "woe is me" mentality and be grumpy for the rest of their recovery phase. Stoics, on the other hand, do not dwell on their misfortune and instead use the time they now have (because they do not have to work) to do something productive. That can be reading books, writing, etc. They try to reframe the event as a means for personal growth.

In short, Stoics do not let adverse events ruin their peace of mind. Instead, they try to make the most out of the situation.

## Respond Differently

"External things are not the problem. It's your assessment of them. Which you can erase right now." – Marcus Aurelius

The Stoic way of life has found its way into modern psychology. For instance, the famous Cognitive Behavioral Therapy (CBT) is based on the concept that our thoughts (cognition), feelings (emotion), and actions (behavior) are all interconnected. It goes like this: thoughts influence feelings and feelings influence behavior. Now we know that modern psychological science proves that Stoicism works.

In many ways, our thoughts determine how we experience reality. For instance, one person may be a nervous wreck when asked to sing on the stage, whereas the other person would grab the microphone and hop right on to the beat. For two people who experience the same hardship, how they assess the situation determines how they feel and behave.

The best way to achieve psychological wellbeing, one should monitor their own inner critic towards greater optimism. Remember that it is not the event itself that creates a negative experience, it is how you perceive it.

## Put Effort In Everything You Do

"Let us prepare our minds as if we'd come to the very end of life. Let us postpone anything. Let us postpone anything. Let us balance life's books each day… The one who puts the finishing touches on their life each day is never short of time." – Seneca

"Keep death and exile before your eyes each day, along with everything that seems terrible – by doing so, you'll never have a base thought nor will you have excessive desire." – Epictetus

In many philosophies, "Memento Mori" is an important concept for both the Stoics and the Existentialists. It basically means "remember that you will die," Morbid? Probably. But this is the stark reality that we all have to acknowledge. Our time on this planet is but a fleeting moment. Seneca and Epictetus understood this very well as they firmly believed that contemplating one's mortality can compel one to be grateful and take more virtuous actions.

By reminding ourselves of our inevitable demise, we learn to appreciate what we have while we still have it. Even with few material possessions, you can still appreciate the good health and wellbeing you have, while you still have them.

By keeping in mind the fact that you are not immortal, you tend to have a better idea of what really matters. The whole idea can be simplified into one short advice: You could get hit by a bus tomorrow. Morbid? True. Still, the point this advice is trying to make is that you should live today as if it's your last day. We all have things to worry about but don't fuss about the small things.

## Virtue is Paramount

It is worth repeating the fact that Stoics should only concern themselves with the question of virtue. The excellence of character is more important than wealth, or even health. The Stoics believe that so long as they behave and think virtuously, there is no need to concern themselves with the influence of external events that they cannot control. Whether or not people are impolite or you experience a series of unfortunate events, it does not matter. What matters is that you respond in a virtuous way. If you do, you are leading a good life.

# Chapter 3: The History of Stoicism

In the previous chapter, we looked at some of the greatest Stoic philosophers and how exactly they contributed to Stoicism in summary. Here, we will study these ancient Stoic philosophers in depth.

For the Stoics, the ultimate goal of our life is "Eudaimonia," which is a state of contentment and flourishing. This can be achieved by living in accordance with nature, as all animals should. Living with nature entails fulfilling your role in the cosmos which is related to the notions of fate and providence and living as a human. Since we are different from animals because we have the capacity for reasoning, we must use this capacity to act accordingly.

Basically, we must act rationally and not be led around by our passion. External circumstances should be viewed objectively, as in neither good nor bad. Therefore, it is best that we are indifferent to them. The entire point of Eudaimonia and the methods to reach it have been developed over the course of human history. Here, we will go briefly over the golden era of stoicism, which is between 300 BC and 200 AD. We will divide this time into three periods: the early, middle, and late stoa. Because the only source in existence about stoicism only dates back to the late stoa period. This is the most well-known of them all.

## Early Stoa (300 – 100 BC) – Zeno, Cleanthes, and Chrysippus

The school of stoicism was founded by Zeno of Citium around 300 BC in Athens. He opposed the school of Epicureanism, which was popular back then. It was founded by Epicurus, who held a more materialistic view of the world. He believed in an accidental nature and a materialistic world, driven only by pain and pleasure. In contrast, Zeno developed his own school of stoicism, which was inspired by many other schools such as Cynicism. Zeno prioritized virtue and simplicity. After recovering from the shipwreck and attending lectures from great philosophers of his time, he started teaching from the Stoa Poikile at the center of Athens. This stoa was a covered colonnade and publicly assessable. From this name, Zeno found the name of his philosophy. Zeno laid the foundation of stoicism and had a powerful influence in the school. He continued maintaining the distinction of the stoic philosophy in three main areas: ethics, physics, and logic. Today, stoicism emphasizes the most on ethics, even though Zeno argued that ethics should always be supported by logic and physics.

Zeno was succeeded by Cleanthes, his pupil, who added a little teaching of his own in addition to following Zeno's teachings. The next leader of the school of stoicism was Chrysippus of Soli, who contributed a lot to the school. He further developed the three parts of philosophy (ethics, physics, and logic). By solidifying and expanding what Zeno had taught, Chrysippus made sure that stoicism was one of the strongest philosophies in history. After that, the school was led by Zeno of Tarsus, Diogenes of Babylon, and Antipater of Tarsus.

## Middle Stoa (100 BC – 0) – Panaetius, Posidonius, Cicero, and Cato

Around 100 BC, stoicism began to shift from Athens to Rhodos and Rome. The seventh scholar, Panaetius, was more flexible in his beliefs than Zeno, who was strict. His contribution was in the form of the simplification of the stoic ideas on physics. He was not as interested in logic in the school of stoicism. This shifted the stoic philosophy closer to Neoplatonism, not to mention making it more assessable to the public. He also brought Stoicism to Rome. Panaetius is considered to be the last scholar because the middle stoa was more elastic, as well as the differences in opinions. After that, there was no longer a unified and undisputed school of stoicism. Still, the Stoic philosophy proves to be able to withstand the test of time as it is more relevant than ever.

Posidonius further reinforced Panaetius' ideas and moved stoicism even closer to Plato and Aristotle, which could be considered to be a Neoplatonist. In Rome, Cicero, and Cato the younger adopted stoicism. Cato, known for his uncompromising moral integrity and his austere way of life, is considered to be the symbol of absolute morality and stoicism. He seems to be associated closer to the teachings of Zeno and Chrysippus than the more flexible philosophy of Panaetius and Posidonius.

## Late Stoa (0 – 200 AD) – Seneca, Epictetus, and Aurelius

During the Roman imperial period, the Stoic philosophers were primarily interested in the questions of ethics. Logics and physics did not receive as much attention anymore. We know much from stoicism from the late stoa as their original writings have survived until today. One of these writings is from Seneca, who used the uniqueness of day-to-day situations to discuss moral issues. Seneca was widely praised for his personalized writing on the school of philosophy and his book Epistulae is still widely known today. If you wish to start studying

Stoicism, we recommend you read Epictetus' handbook. Epictetus was born a slave and provided many insights into stoicism. On the other spectrum, we have Marcus Aurelius who was the Roman emperor. His most prominent work is Ta Eis Heauton (To himself), which he wrote as a personal journal during his military campaign in Germania. Now, it is published under the title "Meditations." This book is the most read and it discussed stoicism extensively, not to mention inspiring people around the world to this day. Concepts such as self-discipline, reason, and world citizenship are still relevant today. Meditations are also used as the main source of personal improvement and growth, arousing renewed interest in stoicism recently. This book is considered to be the last major work from the late stoa.

## In Summary

In short, stoicism has a long history and it withstood the test of time. From great philosophers such as Zeno, all the way to Marcus Aurelius, this school of philosophy has developed well and proven itself to be useful and timeless. It is useful for people from all walks of life, from slaves to emperors. It served Epictetus (a slave) and Marcus (an emperor) well, so this philosophy applies to everyone. While the foundation of Stoicism remained the same, the middle stoa changed it from the eccentric to the eclectic. In the end, the late stoa writers such as Epictetus and Marcus Aurelius gave us many indispensable insights into stoicism.

# Chapter 4: Stoicism and Happiness

Zeno of Cyprus, the founder of Stoicism, was shipwrecked and stranded in Athens. Back then, and even now, this is considered to be a very unfortunate incident. Unlike us, he did not have access to help or much of anything else. For him, it was a devastating incident which could have been the end of his life. Despite that, he remained unfazed. He did not expect anything good to happen.

After losing everything and now not having much else to do, he simply wandered into a bookshop. There, he found the teaching of Socrates that captivated him instantly. After that, he studied with many great philosophers of his time and decided to impart his wisdom on those who wished to learn from him.

This is where the philosophy of stoicism was born. His wisdom was so well-received that both slaves and kings alike implemented it into their lives. He once joked that he made a prosperous voyage when he suffered shipwreck.

However, stoicism does not end there, as a simple footnote in history. Even centuries later, the philosophy remains more relevant than ever in modern society. If anything, life nowadays is even more chaotic than it once was hundreds of years ago. Therefore, there is no better way to find order within chaos than by starting to simplify things in our lives. In this chapter, we will discuss some of the ways you can achieve happiness through practical exercises. You can implement these seamlessly into your life and they are useful for both Stoics and non-stoics alike.

What we will cover here is not some strange ritual, either. It does not involve spirituality. We focus on simple habits to increase your happiness without the use of any equipment.

## A View From Above

This activity is intended to stop your worries by reminding you how insignificant you really are in the grand scheme of things. There is no way you can mess things up that badly on that scale. In other words, this activity helps you to see the bigger picture. Basically, you use your imagination to try and see yourself from a distant standpoint.

There are a few ways you can do this:

## Meditation

There are many forms of meditation, and some people even do it for extended periods of time. However, we want to focus on the activity being practical. Just by meditating for five to ten minutes will suffice. We will cover meditation and mindfulness in the next chapter.

## Do It Yourself

This can be a better alternative as it does not require the use of any equipment. You can do it anywhere. However, for the best experience, we recommend you visit the park or beach. To give yourself the magnitude of the whole universe and how insignificant you are in relation to it, you can start by visualizing a bird's eye view from the sky, or much further to a distant nebula if you wish. From that viewpoint, work your way down. For example, if you start from the sky, then come closer to the world and the people living in it. Observe everything that happens, such as first kisses, discoveries, wars, learning, traffic jams, artistic creations, etc. Observe them as they happen, but refrain yourself from judging them. Remember that many of the things you think are important are actually relatively important. Some care about it, some don't. The same can be said about you. You are only relatively important. Some care about you, others do not.

If you wish to take it a step further, you can imagine yourself in a world frozen in time. Imagine yourself walking through this world and how still everything is. Observe and enjoy that moment of stillness and tranquility.

Alternatively, you can imagine yourself at a different point in time. Imagine life in the medieval era, or in the futuristic era. This can help you remember the fact that you did not exist at a certain point in time and, at some point in the future, you will not exist.

## Contemplate the Ideal Man

This activity is intended to give you motivation for change to become an ideal individual – the best you. Because we can never become perfect, you can only improve upon yourself gradually.

For this exercise, think about the qualities that an ideal person would have. To help your visualization, let us assume that the Roman and Greek status represent the ideal person. Of course, we will not focus on the physical manifestation, but instead the psychological aspects.

What qualities make a person ideal? In many ways, this is a difficult question to answer. It can be easier to instead focus on what an ideal person would do in the situation. From the actions they take, we can then determine their inner qualities. Hopefully, we can start to emulate them. Of course, an ideal person is nothing more than an image, but our goal here is to strive to be as close to that person as possible.

You can solidify the effectiveness of this exercise further by creating a list of real role models, past or present. Then, conduct a thorough analysis of all those individuals to find the qualities that make them ideal. Find the best qualities, and discard the rest.

Alternatively, you can learn the virtues of an ideal individual by knowing what not to do. You just contemplate the actions of the worst type of person imaginable, and then just avoid being that person.

## Cultivating Philanthropy

Before we get into the exercise, let us define philanthropy. It is the desire to promote the welfare of others. Contrary to popular belief, money is not the only means to become a philanthropist. In reality, anyone can be one. All that is needed is the right attitude towards others.

The problem is that we believe that we live in a series of spheres, one inside another. Think of the famous Russian Babushka doll. Each sphere represents a larger distance from our real selves.

So, how do you cultivate philanthropy? The goal here is to bring everyone closer, therefore, merging all of these spheres or layers together. Consider your family to be an extension of yourself. Think of your neighbors as your family. That way, you cultivate a virtue of caring for others, which is key to a virtuous life.

This requires a major change in perspective and it will take a lot of effort. It does have its advantages though. First and most importantly, you will not become overly attached to any particular individual. This prevents you from being devastated in case of loss of friends or their death. Another benefit here is that you will have a larger circle of friends. This exposes you to more culture and viewpoints, meaning the greater the opportunity for learning.

In addition to considering others to be closer to you, there are other things you can do to cultivate the philanthropist within you. You can strike up a pleasant conversation with a stranger, or let your close friend know that you consider them to be a part of your family and that they can and should rely on you.

## **Self Retreat**

Many of us have very good reasons why we would like to travel the world. The most common reason is "to escape and disappear." This is to say that we want to go somewhere where we feel disconnected from the troubles and stress of our everyday routines. So, you may find the idea of a beach in a remote tropical area appealing if you live in the city or you think the bright and colorful lights of the city strikes your fancy better if you live in a remote area. You take yourself to a place where nothing reminds you of your worries. You can achieve peace of mind this way, but this is deeply unphilosophical. You do not need to take a month's vacation and spend a hundred thousand dollars at a remote island to experience mental tranquility. Peace of mind and freedom are some of the things that come from within. If you run away from what troubles you, you are running away from yourself. Unfortunately, you cannot run away from yourself.

There is a cheaper way to find mental tranquility. Instead of traveling outside your country to some remote location, just travel inside your mind, especially if you need peace of mind or freedom. The freest place is inside your own mind. You can choose to be different right here and now. There is no need to travel to find yourself. All you need is about ten minutes a day to shut the outside world out and allow yourself to look inside your own mind.

"People seek retreats for themselves in the countryside, by the seashore, in the hills, and you too have made it your habit to long for that above all else. But this is altogether unphilosophical, when it is possible for you to retreat into yourself whenever you please; for nowhere can one retreat into greater peace or freedom from care than within one's own soul, especially when a person has things within him that he merely has to look at to recover from that moment of perfect ease of mind (and by ease of mind I mean nothing other than having one's mind in good order). So constantly, grant yourself this retreat and so renew yourself; but keep within you concise and basic precepts that will be enough, at first encounter, to cleanse you from all distress and to send you back without discontent of the life to which you will return." – Marcus Aurelius

There was a video about a prisoner who was sentenced to prison for life. Realizing that he would spend the rest of his days locked in a cell, he started discussing how he could escape it. Not by breaking out, of course. He had a more philosophical pursuit and so he started reading and thinking. After all, since this was his life now, he might as well make use of the time he had left to work on becoming a better person. Now, he does not let the four walls of his cell trap his mind. But what about us? Our body is free, but can we say the same for our mind? It is possible that every one of us is mentally trapped in some way. Some are depressed, for instance.

There are a few things you should keep in mind when you want to go on a self retreat. First, know that your experiences of the events are dictated by how you feel about them, not by the events themselves. Second, know that everything is changing all the time, so there is no point in stressing about it because you cannot do anything about it anyway. Finally, your life is limited, so there is no point fussing all the time.

Other than just retreating into your mind, we have two other activities you should try out. Now, if you have a hard time getting inside your own head, you can visit Calm.com. The website has tools you can use to help you relax before starting this journey. If you want to make this challenging, you can try and practice self retreat in non-ideal situations. It can be when you are watching TV with someone else or perhaps taking the journey while in public transport.

## The Stripping Method

Every single situation has many layers, similar to an onion. To get to the heart of the problem, you need to peel away these layers, which are the things that we bring to the situation, not the issue itself. You can only act according to an ethical framework only when you consider the core issues without the unimportant layers. What does that mean?

Simply put, when you need to solve a problem, you focus on getting the job done. Don't consider your reputation or whatever personal advantage you think you can get out of it. So, ask yourself a few questions.

"What value does this situation bring to everyone?" In many cases, the answer is "none."

"What type of qualities does this situation require?" If you check all of the boxes, then great! If not, then use this situation as an opportunity to develop them.

For instance, many of us struggle in finding a direction in life as we are growing up. We do not really know what we want to do with our lives. We may have some faint ideas, but we still do not feel that we should pursue them. If we strip this question down to its core, we are lost not mainly because we do not know what we can do that would be fulfilling and meaningful. We are struggling to find meaning in our lives. Meaningful pursuits do not always involve monetization, although you may find the perfect career if it is meaningful and you feel passionate about it and can monetize it.

We have already established that material possessions should only serve to further enhance your peace of mind. You do not need them to achieve mental tranquility. When finding meaningful pursuits, you should disregard wealth, title, and other's expectations. That way, you won't be dragged into leading a life that is far from who you really are.

So, ask yourself what you would do if money is not something you need to worry about. Be honest with yourself when answering this question and then go and do that.

## Negative Visualization

Before we get into this, we need to understand what Hedonic Adaptation is. It is the phenomenon in which we get used to the things we have and then start to take them for granted. For instance, when you buy a new phone, you treat it as if it is a fragile object. You would not even dare to drop it from a centimeter high. After having it for a year, you would not even think twice about throwing it across the room into your bed. This also applies to your relationships, which makes Hedonic Adaptation very dangerous.

For instance, a couple falls madly in love with each other and gets married. Everyone can see how much they love each other. They are inseparable. Even when they are not together, they send sweet, romantic texts back and forth ceaselessly. All is good, until about five years into the relationship. They are not together as often, and even when they are, they do not talk to each other much, let alone show signs of affection. The texts are few and far between. Eventually, they divorce. This is the effect of Hedonic Adaptation in a relationship. That is not to say that every single relationship follows this route, but we want to point out what happens if you do not maintain it. Certain things may be important to you, but after a few months or years, they don't seem to be as relevant. That is how we feel. Until we lose it again, do we understand just how much something is worth to us.

So, how do we combat Hedonic Adaptation? Through negative visualization.

Negative visualization is an exercise intended to remind us of how lucky we are even with what little we have. As the name suggests, you just have to think about the bad things that have happened or the good things that have not. You can also decide the scale of the event:

- Losing all your possessions
- Never having met your soulmate
- The death of a loved one
- Losing a limb(s), sight, or hearing

You can also think about how things will go wrong as you are about to do them. You may argue that this kind of pessimistic thinking is counterintuitive to a happy and peaceful life. In reality, it can greatly alter your perspective. You suddenly become happy with the things that you have and all the bad things that did not happen.

If you are not faint-hearted, you can try and imagine how things could go very wrong when you are doing or about to do them. If you are traveling by plane, imagine that it will malfunction and crash. If that is too morbid, consider imagining having been born in the past era when all the things you take for granted had not been invented yet, and how you would miss them.

## Physical Self-Control Training

This exercise is to discipline our mind by purposefully going through physical hardships and going without the things we enjoy. You can say that this is a practical version of negative visualization because you put yourself through the hardship. This training has two purposes:

- To prepare ourselves for physical hardships well in advance or for when we suddenly lose everything
- To train ourselves not to yearn for things that are outside our control. Remember, we can only control our own thoughts and actions.

Remember that you should always grasp everything you get in life loosely. Never become too attached to anything as you may lose it one day. Think of sand. You cannot hold sand tightly because it will slip between your fingers and escape your grasp. So, you can subject yourself through physical self-control training by:

- Not eating anything for a period of time

- Going out in the rainy weather without an umbrella
- For a week, change something in your daily routine to make your day less convenient, straightforward, or uncomfortable
- Try to survive without the internet for a period of time (It's harder than you think!)

It is best to view everything as transient. Everything you own, and even you, will no longer exist one day. You become less attached to your own car if you borrowed it from someone. So, see everything as if it was on a loan. When you lose something, tell yourself that you have not lost it. Instead, say that you have given it back.

## Don't Outsource Your Happiness

"I have often wondered how it is that every man loves himself more than all the rest of men, but yet sets less value on his own opinions of himself than on the opinions of others." – Marcus Aurelius

Many things that we do stem from the fact that we want to be liked and accepted. This is because we are social creatures so socializing and being accepted are important to us. These primal needs guide our actions and are often the sole reason why people fall into depression. Disapproval from our social group makes us feel incompetent and detached. Back then, this could result in exile and eventual death in the wilderness. Today, it still holds true. How much time and effort do you spend trying to appeal to others? What does that cost us?

You may be familiar with this quote, "We spend money we don't have, to buy things we don't need, to impress people we don't like." Let's be real here. We all want others to perceive us in a positive light. So, our career and lifestyle choices are based on how we want others to see us rather than what we really want or what is best for us. This is one of the reasons why we all are prisoners in our own mind.

We mentioned earlier in the book that we should only focus on things that we can control. This is what we should strive for. To appeal to everyone is to appeal to no one. You cannot control what others think of you, no matter how hard you try. So, why care about them at all? The Roman statesman Cato led a life that was independent of the opinions of others. So, what did he do? He threw caution to the wind and wore the most hideous and outlandish outfits, and walked around barefooted. Of course, the public reacted negatively, throwing shame and profanity at him. He remained steadfast. It was his way of accustoming himself to be ashamed so that he could endure it when he was ridiculed when he deserved it. It was also his way of despising all sorts of disgrace because he knew what they felt like.

Through this, Cato was able to stand up to Julius Caesar, whom he believed to have too much power. By subjecting himself to public shaming, he honed his mental resilience and was able to make big decisions when they counted, without the fear of disapproval.

We can learn much from him. It is much better for us to live our own lives, on our own terms, and ignore the opinions of others. So, never outsource your happiness.

## On the Pursuit of Status

Even though he had composed many famous pieces, the French philosopher Denis Diderot spent a large portion of his life in poverty. Unlike many of us, and similar to many other Enlightenment thinkers of his time, Diderot did not care for material possessions. That was until he received a brand new scarlet robe as a gift from his friend.

The robe was absolutely beautiful, so much so that Diderot treasured it above everything else. However, he realized that the robe was so out of place with everything else in his home. Only his robe was this grand, and he had no other objects to match.

So, what did he do? He went on to replace everything that he owned. His straw chair was replaced with a leather one. A large mirror now took over the mantle of his fireplace. A writing desk now occupied the vacant corner of his house. As you might have guessed, Diderot went into debt very quickly. In his essay titled "Regrets for My Old Dressing Gown," he said that he was the absolute master of his old robe. But now, he had become the slave of the new one.

His misfortune gave the name to a phenomenon known as the Diderot Effect. From what we learned from Diderot, we can say that the acquisition of a new possession is not a singular event. It always leads to more and more. Every single new purchase creates a spiral of consumption that just pushes you to buy more things.

### The Diderot Effect

The Diderot Effect is a social phenomenon that points out much of what modern consumerism has become. Many savvy marketers tend to bundle products up together, which happen to complement each other and then sell them to us at a price so compelling that it is nigh impossible to refuse. A single purchase can lead to many, many bad purchase decisions.

Diderot showed us what would happen if we followed up an innocent purchase with many mindless purchases. Still, it is difficult to suppress this consumption pattern. We are only scratching the surface here. We need to examine Diderot's misfortune closely if we want to understand our true challenge.

In his essay, Diderot did not care much for material possessions until he got the new robe. Initially, he did not see how they represent the inherent value and worth of a person. This is what he wrote:

"I can bear the sight of a peasant woman without disgust. That piece of simple cloth that covers her head, the hair that sparsely falls across her cheeks, those tattered rags that half cover her, that poor short petticoat that doesn't cover half her legs, her naked feet covered with muck cannot wound me. It is the image of a state I respect; its the ensemble of the lack of grace of a necessary and unfortunate condition for which I have pity."

After he got his new robe, his view changed drastically. It became a part of his identity. This led him to believe that every other object in his home must reflect his worth, and so he went on a spending spree that buried him in debt. And so he wrote:

"The poor man may take his ease without thinking of appearances, but the rich man is always under a strain."

So how did a robe cause Diderot so much pain?

**What We Really Want**

Diderot was actually correct about how material possessions are intertwined with our identity. The richer we become, the more things become a way of expressing ourselves. Clothes that we wear no longer only cover our skin, but also reflect our social standing and taste.

Geoffrey Miller who is an evolutionary psychologist wrote a book titled "Spent" the following about one of the main reasons why we buy things:

"Humans evolved in small social groups in which image and status were all-important, not only for survival, but for attracting mates, impressing friends, and rearing children. Today we ornament ourselves with goods and services more to make an impression on other people's minds than to enjoy owning a chunk of matter — a fact that renders 'materialism' a profoundly misleading term for much of consumption. Many products are signals first and material objects second. Our vast social-primate brains evolved to pursue one central social goal: to look good in the eyes of others."

It is ironic that we continue to buy more and more things to signal virtue. The reality is that the pursuit of status is actually something that only individuals with low-status do. Only those with low self-worth would care about how others perceive them, so they tend to chase after someone's approval. This is why we chase after possessions.

This also explains why large corporations sunk a lot of money into establishing their branding. Take the iPhone and BMW, for example. They advertise to everyone regardless of their income level. Their main goal is not to sell you their product, not directly anyway. They want you to believe in the identity and value of their products. It is not just an object, but a status symbol. Only a few can afford this luxury, and so people flock to buy those products, believing that these items signal their status.

**The Pursuit of Status**

It is funny when you think about it. Many of us are unhappy about our own situation, and yet we have never been richer throughout history. The problem is in the nature of the game.

By definition, status is hierarchical. Both in the animal kingdom and ours, there can only be one top dog who can get the best out of everything. This means, to climb up the social hierarchy, someone has to go down. This makes the pursuit of status a zero-sum game. Your gain is someone's loss. If we want to have more than our neighbor, we will never have enough. This is not a game with an end. If you want to move up to the top, you need to push everyone else down. This is an impossible task. All you can do here is just maintain your position. So, what do we do?

You may think that the best thing to do is to forego this game altogether. Unfortunately, this may not work out for you. Social hierarchy is a deeply-rooted concept in history and it is critical to our ancestors. It helped determine who got the first choice of mate and meat. Our ancestors purposefully did this so that the most important people in the group continued to protect and guide them. Those people bore the responsibility of protecting others, in return for the privilege they enjoyed. While we no longer need such protection, status still serves the same purpose. In this regard, we have not evolved much at all.

Thankfully, the game of status does not have to be played this way. Even though we are biologically inclined to chase status, it does not mean that you have to buy more things. A larger house may mean that you have to spend more than half of your life working. The same can be applied to everything else with varying degrees.

Everything costs time and money to acquire, but they often do not have that much intrinsic value. Instead, why don't we pursue other activities that still signal at our value, but also have an inherent value? Here are some ideas:

- Work out at the gym: One of the main reasons people work out at the gym is so they can look better and they can tell others about it. In addition to having a fit body that you can be proud of, you also have the added benefit of being healthy.
- Teaching or helping others: They say that the best way to make yourself happy is by helping others. When you help other people learn something, it is a demonstration of expertise. You show them your status as an expert in that subject matter, at least relatively. This is also a great opportunity for you to hone your skills and refine your own understanding.

Jim Rohn once said that the best reward in becoming a millionaire is not the money that you make, but rather the kind of person you have to be in order to become one.

To sum it up, it is really easy for us to get lost chasing after more and more things without stopping to consider what we really want. This is the danger of mindless consumption. Most of the time, all we get are the substitutes or replicas of what we really desire. It will take time, effort, honesty, and reflection to figure out what we want in life.

So, before you embark on your next pursuit for status, stop and take some time to think. From what Diderot has taught us, it can be very costly if you chase the wrong thing.

## Forego Ego and Vanity

"Throw out your conceited opinions, for it is impossible for a person to begin to learn what he thinks he already knows." – Epictetus

Epictetus faced some challenges as a teacher because his students said that they wanted to be taught, but believed that they knew everything deep down. If you are a teacher and lecturer, perhaps you know about this all too well. It is all about ego and arrogance. We think that we have learned enough and are better than other people in the room.

This kind of thinking is dangerous, even more so today.

The information we have today is not enough to solve problems in the future, not to mention that it can be an obstacle for sharper thinking. We live in an age where a bad decision can literally ruin your entire life. Even in ancient times, Marcus Aurelius said that the universe is changing, and life is just an opinion.

You can think of this as a positive feedback loop, in which the result amplifies the cause, which then amplifies the result and so on. When you are well-versed in any field, you know exactly where you are lacking. You may be good at math, but literature is way outside your comfort zone. Those who are ignorant do not know where they are lacking, so they assume that they know everything. This prevents them from learning anything new, which continues the vicious cycle. In any problem-solving process, the first thing you must do is acknowledge that the problem is real. The same applies to personal growth. You need to recognize that you can improve upon yourself before you can start improving your inner qualities.

That is why many brilliant minds today spend a lot of time learning by various means. They know that there is always something new they can learn.

## On the Importance of Staying a Student

It is natural for us to become and remain complacent.

After taking our time going through school and college to acquire the knowledge and skills necessary, we believe that we do not need to grow further. We feel justified in resting because we develop a sense of competence and accomplishment. We believe that we have arrived at our destination, even though this is only a rest stop.

This is a very dangerous mindset to have nowadays. We often never have enough information to make decisions to solve tomorrow's problems. The lack of information proves to be obstacles for future development since our fixed paradigms stop us from developing new perspectives.

We would not have developed as a race as we have today if we did not have an evolution on our side. Everything evolves and develops based on the circumstances around it. Humans are the same way, too. To prevent us from making bad decisions or being lost in the ever-changing societies, we need to keep evolving.

How do we keep up with the changes? Complacency is another form of procrastination we talked about. It prevents us from learning new things. We do not know how we have stagnated until it is too late to change.

It seems to be an arduous task to keep working on ourselves for our whole life. There is one person we can learn from, and that person is Frank Shamrock.

**Frank Shamrock**

First, let us take a look at mixed martial arts. It is one of the most popular and fastest evolving sports. It uses the best and most effective techniques from every single fighting style. If you want to be successful in this sport, you need to learn how to adapt and respond to recent developments.

Frank Shamrock understands that very well. He holds his place as a reigning champion throughout his career. He manages to stay on top of everyone. Considering how fierce the competition is in this field, it is incredible how he maintains his position.

He achieved this feat by becoming a student of the game. Shamrock uses a system called "Plus, Minus, and Equals." Ryan Holiday explained in a book titled "Ego Is the Enemy" that Shamrock believed that a fighter needs someone better to learn from if they want to become better. A fighter also needs someone weaker or lesser than them that they can teach, and also another person that is equal to them that they can challenge themselves against.

By having these three individuals, Shamrock is able to get real and constant feedback about what he knows and doesn't know, from every perspective. It helps keep him grounded, preventing him from developing an ego. Frank Shamrock said, "false ideas about yourself destroy you." So, let us break down his system.

**Plus: Have Someone to Learn From**

"If you cannot see where you are going, ask someone who has been there before." – J. Loren Norris

The only thing preventing us from growing is the belief that we no longer need to grow. Thinking that we know everything that we need to is lethal to our professional and personal life. This is something that some college students think after graduation. They believe that a paper tied up in a fancy red ribbon is going to get then a six-digit income. We all know how well that works for them. Spending more than twenty years in schools and college is not going to be enough. We need to learn much more than that.

Having a mentor or coach who is experienced in the field will be immensely useful as they can prevent us from falling into that kind of thinking. It puts your ego down because the student knows very well that they are not better than the master he is under.

Take a look at Alexander the Great. He had Aristotle as a tutor, from whom he learned governance and ethics before he went on to establish his empire. Helen Keller had Anna Sullivan as her tutor, who taught her how to read and write. Michael Jordan had Phil Jackson and Dean Smith to help him win.

No matter who you are, no matter what your talent and abilities are, there is always someone out there who can help you improve. They see the potential inside us as well as the mistakes we have.

The best thing is that there are mentors everywhere. We live in an age where information is accessible and at the tip of our fingers. Courses, books, and podcasts online contain the knowledge and wisdom of great minds throughout the ages. If you look hard enough, you will certainly find someone to learn from. As they say, "when the student is ready, the teacher will appear."

## Minus: Have Someone to Teach

"No one learns as much about a subject as one who is forced to teach it." – Peter Drucker

It goes without saying that you cannot teach without learning. Otherwise, you'd be a bad teacher.

The phenomenon in which we learn through teaching is called the protégé effect. You can actually learn more by teaching than by learning alone. This has been proven in many studies that found students can recall information more accurately and apply it more effectively if they tutored others.

It actually makes a lot of sense. You need to consolidate your knowledge and think about the topic from multiple angles before you can teach someone about the subject matter. You always learn something new about it when you need to deconstruct a topic and reformulate it so others can understand.

"If you can't explain it simply, you don't understand it well enough." – Albert Einstein

Jim Rohn also said that you are the average of the five people you spend the most time with. This points out the fact that you do not need to worry about finding and being with people who are better than you. Learning opportunities are everywhere.

**Equal: Have Someone to Challenge**

"The healthiest competition occurs when average people win by putting above average effort." – Colin Powell

If you have been following sports, you know that some of the greatest achievements are made at the highest level of competition.

Competition pushes us to our limits. It fuels our primal, Darwinian instinct that only the best shall live. It creates a do-or-die mentality that is very useful for us in certain situations. Moreover, you and your competitors can learn a lot from each other. In many cases, most people are not afraid to exchange some tricks and ideas with one another. A fair, healthy competition breeds mutual respect, which creates a starting point for future collaboration.

Therefore, it is essential that you find your scene where you can compete. Ernest Hemingway moved to Paris in the 1920s so that he could join a scene of expatriate writers and artists who lived in the Left Bank. He found his scene where his peers were. Without relocating to Paris, he would never have developed the skills and connections he needed to become a successful writer.

All of the greatest human achievements are not done singlehandedly. You will need someone who can motivate you to push yourself forward in the face of uncertainty and difficulty.

**Always Remain a Student**

We are living in an age where everyone thinks that they know enough. In many ways, we are opinionated rather than informed. For some of us, we stopped learning after school. We ignore the latest developments and will shut everything out, preventing us from learning anything new. It's worth repeating what Epictetus said:

"It is impossible to learn that which one thinks he already knows."

It is alright if you do not know everything. Nobody does. Shamrock's entire career was built on this fact alone. This was his competitive advantage because he understood where he lags behind, and the work he needs to do to fix those problems. Even though he was, in our eyes, on top of the world, he remained a student and kept learning.

We should try to do the same as well.

## Stand Your Ground

"In doing nothing men learn to do evil." – Cato

Throughout his career that was based mainly on compromise, Cato was very stubborn in his beliefs. He was steadfast in a sense that he believed that there were no shades of grey. All vices are the same, and so are the virtues.

You would be right if you think that this is a very high standard. It is true that many things can only be accomplished through compromise. However, we are willing to compromise far from what we should. We forgo our principles just to be tolerated or to gain monetary benefits.

Cato with his ridiculous standards upset both his political allies and opponents because he was immovable. Compromise was not an option for him. He demanded that his family and friends adopt his stance, with no room for flexibility. Adhering to this high standard did not make him the most likable person, but it did give him unshakable authority. Nothing could move his conscience, so he became Rome's moral arbiter of right and wrong.

Of course, you do not need to be like him. You need to stand your ground because if you stand for nothing, you will fall to everything.

# Chapter 5: On Mindfulness Practices

Mental tranquility, or mindfulness, is not easy to accomplish. Being able to be aware of one's own mind and body during stressful situations is essential for Stoics. Developing this takes time and effort, but how does mindfulness relate to Stoicism?

## Stoic Mindfulness

"What thing, out of all those that go to make up our lives, is done better by those who are inattentive? [...] Do you not realize that when once you let your mind go wandering, it is no longer within your power to recall it?" – Epictetus

Ancient Stoics trained themselves to develop a special form of on-going self-awareness, which we describe as "mindfulness," although it is somewhat different from Buddhist meditation practice. Ancient Stoics said that we should always be mindful, living in the moment, and always be aware of the character of our thoughts and actions. This form of mindfulness is called "Prosochê." A French scholar Pierre Hadot extensively documented in the book titled "Philosophy as a Way of Life" of how psychological exercises can be found in the literature of ancient philosophy, especially Stoicism.

"Attention (prosochê) is the fundamental Stoic spiritual attitude. It is a continuous vigilance and presence of mind, self-consciousness which never sleeps, and a constant tension of the spirit. Thanks to this attitude, the philosopher is fully aware of what he does at each instant, and he wills his action fully." – Hadot

To the Stoics, achieving mindfulness through breathing does not make it a helpful exercise, although there are ways to modify it to make it so. It is not about giving the mind a brief break from the daily hectic of life, but rather to focus on our judgments, especially our value judgments and whether we place value on things outside our control. You may not even need to force yourself to change as it can occur just by observance alone. However, meditation also allows you to take a step back from your own train of thoughts and actions, and observe how they carry you mindlessly along, and you can choose to not waste time on them. In many cases, less is more. Quick mindfulness meditation as simple as breathing or meditating can help you save time and energy throughout your day. By toning down the frequency and duration of unnecessary activities and simplifying your life, you can achieve mental tranquility. This should be the first step because you need to sort out your thought process first before you can move on to adapting yourself to other Stoic practices. It starts with self-observation and noticing what you are actually doing from moment to moment, as you are doing it. From there, you can try out meditating.

# Meditation

Meditation has been proven to be the best way to achieve mental tranquility and is practiced widely throughout history in many religions. The entire process is very simple and it should not take you too much time to prepare everything. If you want to reap lasting benefits of meditation, however, you need to dedicate or find a permanent place where you will spend your time meditating. Here, you will learn all the general ideas of a good meditation practice that you can use to get started right away.

## What You Will Need

Although there are several products out there that claim to help you achieve a more mindful or wholesome meditation, you do not need them to successfully reap the benefits of meditation. Here are three main things to get you started:

### A Place to Meditate

Quite obvious, but meditation veterans will tell you that the location is crucial. You need to find a place with enough light (but not too much), open enough to let the fresh air come through, and with enough space, for you to be able to open up. It is worth mentioning that the place should help you feel relaxed even before you begin, so the decoration or the color of the room should also reflect that. One more thing to consider is noise. It should be kept at a minimum level so you will not get distracted.

### A Seat

While there are standing and walking types of meditation, sitting meditation is the most practiced type of meditation and here is where you should start. You need something to rest your body on, but not to the point that you fall asleep. You need to be aware of your body, while still being relaxed. So, sitting is ideal for you. Here, you have a few alternatives:

- **A Chair:** If you are starting out with meditation, or you have back problems, or you find meditation cushions to be uncomfortable, you can use a chair. In fact, you should start off by sitting on a chair first as it helps you to keep your back straight in a sitting position. Keeping your position upright is crucial in any meditation, and the backrest of the chair will help you with that. Of course, once you become more familiar and comfortable with meditation, it may be worth switching to a meditation cushion.

- **A Meditation Cushion:** A meditation cushion is the most common thing that people sit on when they meditate. It is so popular because of the fact that it is the easiest to sit on with an upright position. That, in turn, helps you stay alert and keep the quality of the meditation high. Of course, a meditation cushion does not have a backrest, but when you slump against it, you will lose focus. The meditation cushion forces you to keep your back straight, and maintaining that healthy form as well as keeping you focused on yourself.

- **A Meditation Bench:** If you are tall, have leg problems, or that meditation cushion is just too uncomfortable and counterproductive to your meditation, you might want to give the meditation bench a shot. Just like the meditation cushion, you still need to sit upright without the backrest so you will not have the urge to slump. What makes this different from the meditation cushion is that it absorbs more weight than the cushion, so it takes off the pressure from your legs and makes meditation comfortable for you.

## Timer

A timer is another crucial tool to help you meditate. When you close your eyes and go on a journey of self-discovery that is meditation, it is easy to lose track of time. Having a timer does come in handy, and it is built into most phones. There is really no need for you to buy a physical meditation timer when your phone works just as well. All that you really need from the timer is to tell you when you should stop meditating so you don't have to break away from the trance just to look at the time.

## What to Do

Here is where many beginners stumble. It is not because it is hard to meditate, it is just that they do not know what to do. Many meditation instructions out there are vague at best. Here, we will focus on the two things you need to do:

### How to Sit

You may see different forms of meditation in many places such as in movies or television, or even on posters. With little information given, beginners may be unsure about the proper way to sit down and meditate. It all boils down to personal preference, which is why you see so many different forms. Still, they share some common traits that you should know:

- **The Eyes:** The goal of meditation is to make you focus on yourself. Some types of meditation may say that you need to close your eyes. Others may need you to keep your eyes open. However, it really boils down to personal preference. If you can focus on your breathing better with your eyes closed, then keep them closed. Some may find that keeping their eyes closed would run the risk of them actually falling asleep. You can avoid this by opening your eyes slightly and focusing on a single space in front of you. Again, if this becomes distracting, then keep your eyes closed and try to remain alert.

- **The Head:** When you meditate, look slightly upward. This form opens your body up and helps the body relax. It also takes off some pressure from your neck when you lean your head back a bit. If you have a bad neck posture (slump forward), then this posture can also help you.

- **The Hands:** Again, you will undoubtedly see different positions. Again, you just need to put them wherever they feel most comfortable for you. Some like to intertwine their fingers, some like to put one palm above the others, and some just put them on the leg. Find out whichever works best for you and stick to it.

- **The Back:** The most important thing to keep in mind is that you need to keep your back straight and erect. If you sit on a chair, it is best not to rest against it. Keep an upright posture so you can concentrate easier.

- **The Legs:** Just like your hands, cross them in whatever way that feels the most comfortable to you. Some prefer putting them in a pretzel-like position (or lotus position), but if it becomes uncomfortable for you, just cross them like you normally do.

## What's next?

The one thing that you need to control (and might be the most difficult thing to control) is your attention. In your life, your attention may be scattered to many things at once. Your phone, the conversation, the time, work, and many other things. Meditation challenges you to gather all of your focus and put it all in a single place: your breathing.

Sounds easy enough, right? Probably. Now that you have everything ready, you can start meditating on the following steps.

- **Get Comfortable:** Go to your meditation place, get the timer ready, and don't forget your chair or meditation cushion or meditation bench. It might help you focus if you dim the lights a bit, or just shut them all off so you can focus better.

- **Set Your Timer:** If you are just starting out, then you should go for 5 minutes of meditation. Some go for 10 minutes or even 30 minutes. We recommend that you to start small first. If you are unfamiliar with meditation, you will find that keeping your attention on your breathing for 5 minutes can be difficult.

- **Focus:** Start the timer, and close your eyes and your mouth. Focus on your breathing as it comes in and out. Here, you can focus on any aspects of your breathing. Whatever works best for you, of course. Some focus on how the air enters and exits the nose. Some focus on how it inflates and deflates the lungs. Some focus on the stomach. You can even focus on the sound you make when you breathe. Pacing is also important. Keep it slow and steady. Take slow and deep breaths. Observe the way you breathe, but try your very best to keep your mind empty. This leads to our third step.

- **Keep Your Mind Empty:** Try your best to not think of anything. Focus all of your attention and mind on the breath that you are taking. It is easy to get distracted. Do not worry about how well you do your meditation. Just focus on doing it.If you do get distracted and your mind wanders, do your best to gently guide it back to your breaths. It can be just as easy to become frustrated when your mind wanders constantly, especially if you are just starting out. You tend to lose focus when you exhale because that is more subtle than when you inhale and it can be hard to concentrate on. If you find it hard to concentrate, try counting your breath when you exhale. That way, you can concentrate on your breath when you breathe in, and concentrate on the number when you breathe out. We recommend you count up to 5 and then reset to 0.

## Some Additional Tips

There are also a few more things you need to keep in mind when you meditate so you can reap all the benefits of meditation:

1. **Try to do it first thing in the morning, and before bed:** Not only will you not forget to do it on a daily basis, meditation also serves as the transition from a relaxed state of the body after a restful sleep to the more active state when you get on with your daily life. You can skip the step entirely and launch yourself into the day full of stressful events, but your body may not catch on and you will feel tired. It will also be hard for you to focus when you work. Meditation is a great bedtime routine as well.

2. **Develop a loving attitude:** When you meditate, many things (good and bad) will come up in your mind. Look at them as if they are there to help you. A way to develop positive thinking is by seeing everything in a kind, and loving way.

3. **Don't worry too much about how you're doing it:** Some people become frustrated or worried that they did not meditate properly when they get distracted for a few seconds during their session. The thing is, there is no way you can meditate perfectly. There will be flaws and you will get distracted sometimes. When your mind wanders, gently guide it back to your breathing. You will get better at this as time passes.

4. **Don't ignore whatever comes:** Meditation is also a journey of self-discovery. When you meditate, most of the small and insignificant things will vanish. However, some deeper, more pressing issues tend to arise. These issues are most likely the source of

your anger, anxiety, or frustration. You will recognize them as they come. Although you should just brush it aside when you meditate, it is worth staying with them for a moment. It can be tricky to stay with those thoughts without feeling the negativity, but it can help you pinpoint the source of your sorrow so you can address them later.

5. **Befriend yourself:** As mentioned earlier, meditation is more than just about relaxing. It is also a journey of self-discovery. When you meditate, be aware of your own thoughts. Chances are they are responsible for your behavior. However, observe yourself in a friendly way, and do not criticize yourself too badly. Give yourself some love and try to understand yourself.

6. **Commit:** This is where most beginners fail. They try it once or twice, and then give up and say that meditation does not help them at all. In reality, it does. All it takes is some effort. Develop a habit of meditation on a daily basis, and you will soon notice the difference.

7. **Comfort and alertness:** We talked about this before, but this needs to be stressed again. No matter what type or form of meditation you practice, comfort and alertness should always be a high priority. If you are uncomfortable, it will be hard for you to concentrate. If you are too comfortable, you run the risk of snoozing off. Find that perfect balance where you are comfortable but alert at the same time. In the end, the pose, form, or placements of hands and legs are up to you. You choose which one is the best for you, and stick to it.

8. **Focus:** If you find it hard to focus on your breathing, or want to try something a little bit more difficult and different, then there are other alternatives that you could try out. You can try to focus on a certain part of the body at a time. Be aware of how that body part feels. You can even try to work your way up from your feet up to your head during meditation. Alternatively, you can place your attention on the light in the room. You can even switch up your point of focus on a daily basis. One day, you focus on the sounds, and the next day, you can focus on the light.

9. **When you're done, smile:** Meditation is also the process of giving yourself the attention you need and deserve. In order to develop positive thinking, smile after you have finished your meditation. Be thankful that you allow yourself some quality time to meditate. Give yourself a pat on the shoulder as if to say "Nice job" for sticking to your commitment. Everyone needs some self-love, and there is not much else to do to feed yourself just that.

## Common Mistakes when Meditating

There are many ways to meditate, that much is true. Some aspects of meditation can be modified to fit your own preferences, although many people pay a little too much attention to detail. The most common mistakes people make when they are meditating is the way that they think.

- **Judging the Experience:** When you meditate, the goal is to keep you breathing steadily and your head clear. It is meant to give your head a break, the silence that it deserves. However, it is also the practice of patience and gratitude. We mentioned before how important it is to keep your mind and heart at peace when you meditate. Beginners tend to worry about whether they are doing it right, or that the meditation that they are practicing is a good one. Instead, stop worrying and focus on the fact that you are practicing meditation. Focus on yourself and the stillness of emotions.
- **Props:** There are many of them that can help you focus. However, it is also worth mentioning that you do not need them to meditate. In fact, they might even distract you from meditating. Meditation is all about inner peace, and you do not need external objects to achieve that. That does not mean that props are worthless. Try to keep them to a minimum. Keep the ones that actually keep you awake or focused.
- **Over-complications:** Nowadays, you can find hundreds of meditation techniques that have modern twists on ancient practices. While science has contributed to these modern meditation techniques, it is worth noting that they may lack the spiritual experience. Traditional meditation techniques have been developed and have thousands of years of experience in spiritual growth, and that is what makes them a better choice for serious practitioners. Modern meditation techniques can be fun to try out, but you should stick to the traditional ones.
- **Guided Meditations:** This is a type of meditation which we will discuss later. Basically, it helps beginners and experts alike unlock the key to inner peace easier. However, it is not recommended that you use it every time when you meditate. While helpful in itself, you should learn how to access that place of silence and peace on your own. Otherwise, your own journey is not worthwhile. Of course, that does not mean that you should ditch this meditation altogether. You just need to maintain a healthy balance between guided meditations and solo meditations.
- **Spice things up** Meditation can get repetitive and boring very quickly. When it does, you will find it hard to keep meditating. How do you avoid that? Simple. You can mix things up a bit to keep it interesting. Try meditating with your eyes open, or with soothing ambient music (if you haven't already). If you are feeling adventurous, then you can even try meditating while you are working. All you need to do is to keep your head clear and breathing deep and constant. You do not really need to sit down in a meditating position in order to start meditating. Just make sure that you are comfortable with the environment before you start.

## How to Develop Awareness of Emotions and Thoughts

Your thoughts are your inner dialogue, a conversation between you and you. We have an average of six thousand thoughts a day, which we often repeat to ourselves. In many cases, these thoughts come from past experience or childhood experience. Since then, it has been repeating itself in your head. Because our cognitive abilities do not develop fully until the mid-20s, you can tell how many of these thoughts no longer serve you.

Why should we develop an awareness of our inner dialogue? After all, it seems so effortless to talk to yourself and so insignificant. By controlling how you think about yourself and what is around you, you can start to regulate and choose your own response to any event. This is key to mental tranquility.

Simply put, you want to be aware of what you are saying to yourself inside. That way, you have direct control over your choices, not your emotions. Your happiness and peace of mind depend on this. This is important because your thoughts can activate certain thought processes within you, driven purely by emotions, even painful ones. Your thoughts and the beliefs that drive them cause you to feel a certain way toward something.

Even though external events may cause you to feel or react in a certain way, they actually do not. What you feel is just a result of your mind's interpretation of reality and it tells you how to feel about it. Most of what it tells you is subconscious, coming from the beliefs that you have. These beliefs are also subconscious.

When you control what you think, not allowing your emotions to cloud your judgments, you also control your behavior. This means you can control how your life unfolds to an extent. To begin, we need to develop self-awareness to transform your thoughts.

While controlling your own emotions allows you to have a more rational approach to the situation, you also gain an understanding of the power of emotions. Learning how to use them to your advantage is just as crucial. Emotions are chemical molecules that command circuits of your body. They have a powerful influence on your beliefs, thoughts, and behaviors. Your emotions are indicators.

Just like a GPS, you can tell if you are where you want to be based on your feelings. Your success in overcoming problems depends on your ability to experience emotions and let them tell you from moment to moment as you make decisions.

For instance, when you feel good, joy, happiness, or confidence, it is a sign that your inner drives are met. However, this can be misleading because not all positive emotions mean that you are in the right place. It may work against your highest interest.

On the other hand, negative emotions are indicators that tell you that you are probably not in the right place. They make you feel stressed. Still, important events require you to put yourself through this unpleasant experience. Things such as taking an exam or dealing with an important issue help you grow, perform, and achieve some amazing things.

Therefore, it is critical that you learn how to connect empathically with unpleasant feelings like anxiety, guilt, shame, or hurt. They give you a lot more information about yourself than your positive emotions. They give you a better idea of where you are in relation to where you want to be. For instance, emotions based on fear indicate that you should stop and evaluate what other possible actions or changes that can support your visions or goals better. More often than not, the solution can be as simple as replacing a limiting belief with an energizing one. It may be more challenging because you may need to openly express your emotions to another person authentically without placing the blame on anyone.

We have seven steps to develop your awareness of your feelings and how they are connected to your thoughts.

## Select a Triggering Situation to Process

First, make a list of events that trigger anger in you. Arrange them in order from the least challenging to process to the most challenging. Work on the easiest triggers, one at a time, and move gradually up to the most challenging. Take it slow because it might take you weeks. It requires patience. You need to stretch yourself outside your comfort zone but not so much that you become overwhelmed with the process. If it becomes too emotionally intense, take a break. If this happens, it's probably a good idea to get professional help from a therapist or a counselor.

## Center Yourself in the Present

When you have identified and selected the trigger you wish to reflect on, take a moment and take three to five deep breaths from your diaphragm to allow yourself to relax. Focus on your breathing with your eyes closed. Notice how your body feels from the top of your head to the tip of your toes. Release any tension or tightness.

Then, imagine yourself in a safe place where you can let your guard down. Separate yourself from your emotions or thoughts by reminding yourself that you are the observer who has the creator of these emotions and thoughts. Remind yourself that this is good news as you are in control of your emotions so no one can make you feel a certain way toward something without your permission. Observe your emotions and make a mental note to yourself that anything that you feel results from past experience, from a time when you did not have the ability to know and see yourself and life from different viewpoints. Now that you are capable, you are in charge of your thought processes. You can stop this exercise whenever you want.

## Identify and Feel Your Emotions and Feelings

After relaxing and preparing yourself for this reflective session, start bringing the selected trigger to mind. Remember the list we made earlier? Choose the easiest trigger and recall its most recent occurrence. Then, be aware of how that event makes you feel. Be aware of your sensations without judging. Notice how you feel inside as you take slow, deep breaths. Then, ask yourself, "What am I feeling right now?"

If you feel anger, go down another layer. Find other emotions beneath it. Anger is only a secondary emotion that protects you from feeling emotions associated with vulnerability such as fear, shame, or hurt. So, if you feel anger, ask yourself, "What underlies this anger?"

What emotions and feelings do you feel? Write them down in your philosophical journal and reflect upon them at the end or start of the day.

## Feel and Notice the Location of Any Sensation in Your Body

In addition to anger, also notice how your body feels. Pause and feel each sensation as you feel each emotion. Note down what physical sensations you feel. For each motion that is triggered, ask yourself what your body feels as you imagine the triggering event. Note the location of these physical sensations. Feel that sensation and breathe deeply while placing one or both of your hands on where you feel them in your body. When you do, let go of any impulse to stop, judge, repress, or fix any of your emotions and sensations. Continue to probe them. You may notice that the sensation may be less intense over time. If you feel that anger is your primary emotion, keep asking yourself what else you feel. Try to describe that sensation and record where you feel it.

## Accept Your Feelings

Dissociate yourself from your emotions by telling yourself that you are not your emotions. You are the observer and the emotions are just energy. What you feel is just pockets of energy linked to past wounds. Because you are the decision-maker in your life, you can choose to tap into this painful past through breathing and notice the energy shift, move, and release. You can choose to affirm the power that you have as the decision-maker and accept these painful feelings because it is natural to feel pain because you are human. So, calmly and confidently affirm, "I accept that I am feeling (emotion) at this moment."

Repeat this to yourself silently or aloud: "I can handle this emotion. I am strong and can handle this calmly, easily, wisely."

A great way to gain leverage on negative emotions is by remembering a time when you experienced similar emotions and handled it successfully. Because you have dealt with it once, you can do it again right now and in the future. Tell yourself, "I have handled this emotion in the past. I can do it again today, and in the future." Repeat this affirmation to yourself several times as needed until you feel a change in your emotional state and its intensity. While you are doing this, take slow deep breaths between each repetition. Remember that each time you handle this emotion, you improve your mental resilience. This will strengthen and develop your confidence and your ability to cope with negative emotions. This, in turn, allows you to learn from negative emotions and turn them into assets.

## Identify What You Tell Yourself

Then, notice your thoughts as you picture the triggering event, especially any toxic thinking patterns. Your thoughts always trigger physical sensations and emotions in your body. This is just how our brain works.

Observe these thoughts from a distance, as the objective observer. Again, do not judge your experience. Use this visual. When a disturbing thought surfaces, imagine yourself sitting in a luxurious high-speed train, looking out the window, and nonchalantly observe any upsetting thoughts passing by in a flash outside the window as you sit comfortably in your seat in a safe place. Write down what you tell yourself next to the emotions and physical sensations you went through in the previous steps.

## Connect Empathically

Finally, remind yourself that although other situations or people can cause painful emotions in you, they are not the cause themselves. How you interpret the situation, your self-talk, causes all of these painful emotions you feel such as guilt or frustration, resentment or anger. This is good because if how you interpret external events causes you to feel upset, you can choose to change how you interpret them and empower your confidence and ability to make the right choices.

Remember that being able to control how you interpret external events is really, really good news. That means you are in full control of your emotional responses, thoughts, and actions. You can protect your happiness and peace of mind no matter what the world throws at you. No one can make you feel a certain way toward something unless you allow it.

By understanding this, you can create statements to affirm and validate your experience, like this: "It makes sense that I feel overwhelmed because I'm telling myself that I'll never get this done, this is too much for me, or I cannot handle it."

In short, your thoughts evoke emotions inside of you, and these emotions may tell you something important that you need to know to live your life happily. These emotions may tell you how to best live your life and thrive. When you develop your awareness of these indicators (emotions and sensations), you have a better understanding of the connection between your words or thoughts to your emotions and physical sensations.

When you do, you will realize that you have a lot more control over your thoughts than you may think. You come to find out that just by making a few tweaks in the way you think, you can improve your life considerably. Changing how you experience events in a way that allows you to still remain on the life-enriching course you chose will be the best chance you will ever get in life. Your emotions, especially the painful ones, will be indicators – guides to tell you whether you are on the right path to mental tranquility. When you understand the power of shaping your emotions and how they work with your thoughts, it becomes a lot easier to confront and embrace them instead of avoiding, minimizing, or looking down on them.

In the vast and unforgiving ocean of life, your feelings act as your navigation system. Use them wisely.

# Chapter 6: On Consolidation of Thoughts

"No man was ever wise by chance." – Seneca

We all have many things to do every day, but none of them entail looking into ourselves. This happens to be the most important thing for a Stoic. Through self-reflection, you are forced to question yourself and examine your assumptions of the world. This is how some have found the answers to many of the world's biggest questions.

Having a journal is one of the best ways to maintain mindfulness. Moreover, it helps boost creativity, increases gratitude, and also serves as therapy as you are your own therapist. The benefits are countless. Manyof the world's greatest minds keep a journal with them all the time so that they can record their thoughts and feelings. They are much clearer when you put them into words because you need to consult them for details and formulate phrases to express your true thoughts and feelings.

The Stoics are aware of this. The book titled "Meditations" was a personal journal of Marcus Aurelius who was one of the most powerful men in history. He took the time to record his feelings and observations, during both peace and war times.

While many people have benefited from Marcus' ideas today, it is clear that he benefited the most from his thinking and writing. His journal kept his thoughts clear and held him accountable so he continued to lead a virtuous life when anyone in his position would have become corrupt and a tyrant.

## Philosophical Journal

You may already know the benefits of keeping a journal, but we want to focus on another type of journal. Instead of writing about what happened in your life, you can also take a long hard look at it from a Stoic's perspective. You can use this journal to discover your own shortcomings and then track how you have changed over time. Through constant reflection and conscious efforts put into self-improvements, you can improve your life.

So, start planning your future actions by taking into consideration the ethical framework. From there, write down what happened and see what needs to be changed. This Stoic exercise can be integrated seamlessly if you are already writing a personal journal. All you need to do is record what happened and then try to come up with how you can change based on the event.

Start by keeping a daily philosophical journal and record everyday events for at least one month. For more resources, you can refer to Marcus Aurelius' philosophical journal titled "Meditations."

## Early Morning Reflection

"Cling tooth and nail to the following rule: Not to give in to adversity, never to trust prosperity, and always to take full note of fortune's habit of behaving just as she pleases, treating her as if she were actually going to do everything it is in her power to do. Whatever you have been expecting for some time comes as less of a shock." – Seneca

At the start of your day, make a habit of reflecting. It's more nuanced than you think. It's more than just planning out what you want to do during the day. It's also about priming your mind to react a certain way to the things that may happen throughout the day.

So, be thankful for the fact that you just woke up. We discussed the morbid idea of our mortality back in the first chapter, so smile and be thankful for the fact that you are alive and well. This is the first step.

Then, in addition to planning out the day ahead, plan how you want to embrace your virtues and avoid your vices. Choose a personal strength or philosophical precept that you wish to cultivate, then plan how you wish to incorporate it into the day. As always, expect to face difficulties throughout the day. So, plan ahead on how you want to respond to these events that align with your personal growth goals for the day.

Finally, remind yourself to only worry about the things you can control such as your thoughts and actions. Disregard everything else.

There are other activities you can do here. If you manage to wake up early enough and have plenty of time on your hands, you can go out for a walk and enjoy the morning sun and meditate on how you can develop yourself as a person.

While you are out walking, you can take some time to perform light exercises. You do not need a dumbbell or other fancy equipment. Just simple bodyweight exercises are enough. While you are at it, think of your own mortality and the fact that you will age.

## Bedtime Reflection

In addition to reflecting in the morning and writing a journal about your day, it is a good idea to have a bedtime reflection session. So, replay the entire day mentally and then ask yourself these questions:

- Did my behavior align with my principles?
- Did I treat others in a friendly and considerate manner?
- What voices have I fought?
- Have I made myself a better person through the cultivation of my virtues?

While you are at it, feel free to plan for the next day as well. You can write down a few things you should think about in the morning in your philosophical journal. This links up seamlessly with your early morning routine and your philosophical journal.

Simply put, this activity is all about learning from your mistakes.

In your philosophical journal, you can write down one thing you want to improve the next day, no matter how insignificant it may seem. We want to focus on small but constant improvement. You may be surprised at how much you can change if you keep this up for just a month. Set a small goal and stick to it.

Other than that, remind yourself that today is finished and you can do nothing to change what happened. Accept everything that has happened, good or not.

## How Journaling Leads to a Better Life

The first thing you may recall about Benjamin Franklin is the fact that he is one of the founding fathers of the United States. He helped write the famous United States Constitution and the Declaration of Independence. He defended the American Cause. However, he was more than just a politician. He was also a polymath.

Other than politics, Benjamin Franklin was known as the father of electricity. He was a scientist and inventor. He began experimenting with electricity when he accidentally shocked himself. His curiosity and fascination turned to obsession, which resulted in the invention of the lightning rod that proves useful to today.

Franklin also has his contribution to the world in the literature field. He was an essayist, newspaper publisher, and an author. Some of his works include his own autobiography and Poor Richard's Almanac.

Although he was born into a poor family and only got two years' worth of formal education, what Franklin was able to achieve and contribute was astounding. If there ever was a self-made man, he certainly was one.

One of the things that contributed to his success was his habit of keeping a journal. Franklin had many journals throughout his entire life and used them in ways we could not imagine. While we all know the benefits and importance of keeping a journal, they were not so apparent back then. This made Franklin a different man from other men of his time. By understanding how he used his journals, we can understand what went on in his mind.

## Focus

Franklin was a disciplined man. This is not surprising considering the feats he accomplished. He followed his schedule strictly. As he wrote in "The Autobiography of Benjamin Franklin":

> "The precept of Order requiring that every part of my business should have its allotted time, one page in my little book contained the following scheme of employment for the twenty-four hours of a natural day"

It sounds like your modern-day calendar, doesn't it? You're not wrong. Franklin understood that he only had 24 hours a day, and he wanted to spend them effectively. He knew how important it was to plan how he would use his time. Notably, he also tracked how he used his time and corrected it as needed. As Peter Drucker once said, "what gets measured, gets managed."

This is one of the uses Franklin had for journals. Research shows that keeping a simple to-do list is not as effective as keeping a journal. When you create a specific time for a specific activity, you are more likely to do it when the time comes. If you do not define exactly when you want to do it, you will probably not do it.

Of course, a journal has many uses. There are no specific purposes for having a journal so you can use it for productivity if you struggle to keep one. Having a journal allows you to jot down more details when you write about your activities, compared to a calendar. It is not the most obvious benefit, but it certainly helps you plan out your life.

## Accountability

Franklin talked about self-improvement and lived it, making sure that he was not lying to himself. His desire to improve as a person was crucial to his success. His pursuit of excellence was all-encompassing because he sought to improve mentally, professionally, and morally. He started his moral pursuits at the early age of 20, after which he started adopting other virtuous habits.

Franklin followed thirteen virtues that he believed to be desirable. But unlike others that only preach these virtues, he lived them and tracked his progress. He wrote:

> "My intention being to acquire the habitude of all these virtues, I judg'd it would be well not to distract my attention by attempting the whole at once, but to fix it on one of them at a time; and, when I should be master of that, then to proceed to another, and so on, till I should have gone thro' the thirteen."

The thirteen virtues he tried to acquire were carefully thought out. At the end of each day, Franklin would evaluate himself based on these virtues and marked which virtues he violated. His goal was to keep the number of marks off his journal to a minimum. Therefore, the indicator he used to determine whether he led a life of virtue would be how pristine his journal was. These are his virtues at the age of twenty:

1. Temperance: Eat not to dullness, drink not to elevation.
2. Silence: Speak not but what may benefit others or yourself; avoid trifling conversation.
3. Order: Let all your things have their place; let each part of your business have its time.
4. Resolution: Resolve to perform what you ought; perform without fail what you resolve.
5. Frugality: Make no expense but to do good to others or yourself; i.e., waste nothing.
6. Industry: Lose no time; be always employ'd in something useful; cut off all unnecessary actions.
7. Sincerity: Use no hurtful deceit; think innocently and justly, and, if you speak, speak accordingly.
8. Justice: Wrong none by doing injuries, or omitting the benefits that are your duty.

9. Moderation: Avoid extremes; forbear resenting injuries so much as you think they deserve.
10. Cleanliness: Tolerate no uncleanliness in body, clothes, or habitation.
11. Tranquility: Be not disturbed at trifles, or at accidents common or unavoidable.
12. Chasity: Rarely use venery but for health or offspring, never to dullness, weakness, or the injury of your own or another's peace or reputation.
13. Humility: Imitate Jesus and Socrates.

You may say that these virtues set an impossibly high standard, to which you are absolutely correct. Benjamin Franklin himself did not attain his goal of perfect morality, but he did at least keep the habit of self-improvement. The journal kept him accountable and he did the best he could, which we all should strive toward. Perhaps you can incorporate these virtues into your life as well. The goal is not to follow every one of them to the letter, but rather to give you something to work toward.

## Reflection

While Franklin strived not to waste an hour of his time, he always questioned the value of his work and motives behind his activities, believing that self-reflection must not be ignored.

For example, he had the habit of asking himself two questions every day when he questioned himself whether he had violated any of the thirteen virtues. At the top of his page, he wrote: "What good shall I do this day?" This allowed him to reflect the virtues he must follow and how he could improve upon his past self. At the end of the day, he wrote: "What good have I done today?"

He conducted this integrity report every day. He tracked what he did and when during his working hours, but spent some time at the end of the day asking himself why he did what he did.

He never shied away from answering difficult questions. Many of us spend our journaling hours writing inspirations and affirmations, but Franklin used his journal differently: To track his moral wrongdoings. He recorded every wrongdoing he had committed on the left side of his journal, and what he had done to right the wrong on the right.

Among his moral shortcomings was his tolerance of slavery. He allowed for the sale of slaves to be advertised on the Pennsylvania Gazette, which he owned. He even owned slaves for himself although he was apprehensive of this practice. However, his greatest moral failing was when he agreed to a compromise that resulted in the enshrinement of slavery in the constitution.

Franklin could not right this wrong, but he did do his very best to fix his mistakes even in his elderly age. He eventually became the President of the Society for the Abolition of Slavery, and actively and publicly spoke out against such practice.

## Journaling

Franklin certainly would not have been the person he was without his journals. After studying his life, we can see how keeping a journal gives you a better sense of control over ourselves.

Many of us focus more on how forward-thinking journaling can be. That is certainly alright, but it may not translate into the results we seek. One of the problems with journaling is that we get a sense of accomplishment from writing things down, but that is only therapeutic. It does not mean that we will take action to get the results we desire.

As we mentioned earlier, Franklin did not use the journal to inspire himself. He used it to hold himself accountable for his wrongdoings. His journal compels him to take action – to do the right thing and become a better person. Franklin knows this and took steps to improve himself instead of wishing that he would do better tomorrow.

His journaling was a keystone habit, which allows the power of journaling to manifest further than just being a mindless record of his daily life. His life was heavily based on journaling because this was a habit for him. We can learn much from Franklin's life, especially how he used his journal to learn, reflect, and account for his actions.

More importantly, you need to learn how to record your own story. It may not seem like much for you now, but small and incremental improvements can amount to much in just a month. Over the course of a lifetime, no one knows how much positive influence a journal can bring into your life.

## Keystone Habits

We used the word "keystone" habit in the previous section. What exactly is it? Well, allow us to tell you a story first.

Michael Phelps is perhaps one of the most decorated Olympians of all time. He has won 28 medals in many swimming categories and is the current champion of many world records even though he has now retired. His 80-inch wingspan and flexible ankles made him a better swimmer than a runner. He was a gifted swimmer, but that was not the entire story.

What was not so well-known about his success was the fact that his life has been built on a few habits. They were instilled into him to turn him into a world-class swimmer. Bob Bowman, his swimming coach, knew that Phelps had the potential to be a great swimmer, but for him to become world-class, he needed habits to turn him into the best mental swimmer there was.

Then the 2008 Olympics came about and Bowman was proven correct. Phelps went on to win eight medals in a single Olympics, making him the first person to have ever accomplished such a feat. When Bowman was asked about how Phelps prepared for the Olympics (possibly suspecting that he had a different training regiment, diet plans, etc.) Bowman said:

"If you ask Michael what was going on inside his head before the competition, he would say that he wasn't really thinking about anything. He was just following the program. But that's not the entire story. It's more like his habits have taken over. Everything went according to plan. The warm-up laps were just like he visualized. The stretches went as he planned. His headphones are playing exactly what he expected."

What many of us see as tedious, Bowman saw as essential and indispensable. He then went on to explain that the actual race was just another event in a set of patterns that started earlier that day. The pattern pointed Phelps to nothing but victory, so of course, winning is just a natural extension.

## The Power of Keystone Habits

Habits automate your actions and outcomes, making everything predictable. When our body is on autopilot, we can perform as expected no matter what the environment you are put in is. That matters if every single action counts, especially if you are competing at the highest level like Phelps.

Phelps had many habits incorporated into his routines. He would visualize his perfect race, with each stroke, turn and finish done in perfection, before and after going to bed. His stretching regimen follows a certain pattern, starting with his arms and ending at his ankles. He knows how long his warm-up will take before each race.

Now, it sounds like you need to pick up a lot of habits in order to achieve something amazing. It is not. You see, these habits were not developed one by one. Some habits compound, meaning that they go together. So, if you take up one habit, a few more will follow naturally.

In the book called "The Power of Habit," Charles Duhigg called these habits the keystone habits. Unlike ordinary habits, keystone habits create positive effects that go over into other areas by starting a chain reaction that shifts many other patterns. This transforms everything over time. Think of a keystone habit as a switch that you just flip to cause this chain reaction.

**What A Keystone Habit Looks Like**

A keystone is characterized by its ability to trigger a set of behaviors.

For example: Suppose that you start to track your food to know how many calories you were consuming. Eventually, after seeing the numbers, you start exercising, then reducing your carbohydrates intake. That means that you started to order takeouts less frequently, and started cooking for yourself more and more.

You may pick up all of these habits without realizing it. You may look back one day and be surprised at how such a trivial act of keeping track of your food motivated you to lead a much healthier lifestyle. If you were to take a closer look, you may realize that the process was actually simple.

You become more aware of what you are eating and how many calories you are consuming. After assessing your eating habits, you start going for runs and going to the gym. Then, you think that it makes sense to further complement your efforts by optimizing your diet and starting to eat healthier food. Based on where you live, you may start to learn how to cook your own meals to follow through with your new lifestyle.

So, what we have was a small act of curiosity that led to a series of habits that make you lead a healthier life. A small change can have a drastic effect on your life. For Franklin, his keystone habit of journaling led him down a virtuous life. You can too.

**Building Your Keystone Habit**

You have many options to establish a keystone habit. In reality, it does not matter which action you choose because it does not cause a chain reaction. It is the intent behind the act. As Duhigg writes:

"The power of a keystone habit draws from its ability to change your self-image. Basically, anything can become a keystone habit if it has this power to make you see yourself in a different way."

So, the range of habits is unlimited. Even actions that do not seem connected can yield unexpected benefits. Here are some keystone habits you should pick up:

- Wake up early: If you can, try to sleep earlier so you can get up early. That way, you have an hour or two to yourself which you can use to pursue your hobbies or other activities you are interested in. This can allow you to spend more time reading or working on your passion project. This extra time gives you an edge over your competitors by allowing you to master difficult skills, increasing your sense of possibility and confidence.
- Make your bed: It sounds silly, true, but this simple action can give you a better sense of control. When you tidy up your room, the first thing you should do is tidy the bed, so everything looks easier. Plus, doing this in the morning gives you a little boost in discipline and confidence, allowing you to go on to accomplish other things during the day. This is something that Admiral William McRaven had to do when he was a Navy SEAL. It was his keystone habit. You can find out more in his book "Make Your Bed."
- Meditate: We feel that this is worth mentioning again. There are many benefits associated with meditation, including improved self-awareness, reduction of anxiety, and greater emotional stability. The mental tranquility this brings can help you in decision-making.

So, let us not confine ourselves to specific behaviors. Start getting your life sorted, make your bed, get up early if you can, and you will start seeing the difference. The point is: start doing something that you will eventually enjoy and work from there.

# Chapter 7: Overcoming Negative Emotions

In this chapter, we will discuss how you can deal with negative emotions in the Stoic way.

## Stay Focused

"If a person doesn't know to which port they sail, no wind is favorable." – Seneca

Thanks to modern-day capitalism, we are spoiled for choice. Whether it is food, entertainment, or travel, we have many more options than what people used to a few decades ago. Still, this does not benefit us. When we have so many alternatives, we become stunned by indecision.

This phenomenon is known as the paradox of choice. It is the overload of information when our brain is presented with so much data. Our brain cannot keep up with the amount. When that happens, we often choose to maintain the status quo.

This is one of the main problems we face every day. With so many things to choose from, we do not fully commit to a particular path. We either do everything at once or put off making decisions altogether. This often results in us never really making much progress anywhere.

In this regard, the Stoics focused on purposeful actions. We need to ensure that we do not take action just as a reaction to our circumstances. We need to make sure that our actions have an intention, a purpose.

## Develop an Internal Locus of Control

"Man is disturbed not by things, but by the views he takes of them." – Epictetus

To start things off, you need to know what you can and cannot control. Many things that happen in our lives are outside our realm of control. The stoics know this undeniable truth and instead focus on what they can do to better the situation.

Epictetus was born a slave so it would seem that he had no reason to believe that he had control over anything. Cursed with a broken leg by his master, anyone would guess that he would live and die in poverty.

Anyone would fall into despair in such a situation, but not Epictetus. He saw things differently. Even though his property and even his body were not within his realm of control, he understood that his opinions, desires, and aversions still belonged to him. These were the few things he owned, and he made peace with that.

What about us? We take so many things for granted that we become frustrated very easily. We are so used to the comfort of our own home and technology that even a minor inconvenience can make our face turn red with rage. If the internet chokes for a second, or the traffic is only a minute slower, we would be annoyed if not outright angry.

What causes us to be this angry? From what Epictetus said, it is not the breakdowns or dysfunctions that upset us. This unhappiness stems from choice. We choose to feel angry at these minor inconveniences. We have no one but ourselves to blame for the way we respond to external events that affect our internal state of mind.

Basically, we have the power to be happy no matter what goes on in our lives. It is not the external events that cause us to be unhappy. It is how we feel toward them.

## Guard Your Time

We're tight-fisted with property and money, yet think too little of wasting time, the one thing about which we all should be the toughest misers." – Seneca

Time is a commodity we all spend, and it is a priceless one at that. Unlike other assets, no amount of money can buy us another second of time. Once lost, you cannot regain it. The Stoics understood that well. So, learn how to make the most out of what little time you have.

Those who carelessly throw away their time on insignificant entertainment just for pure pleasure will find themselves at the end of the road with nothing to show for it. Procrastination is dangerous, hence the reason sloth is one of the seven deadly sins. What you put off until tomorrow will come back to bite you. Tomorrow is not always guaranteed, so if you can do it today, do it.

But being resourceful with your time is much more than that. Some people may find themselves giving their time away freely to others. This is just as bad as wasting time. Many of us allow people and other obligations to take up our time too easily. We make promises without giving much thought to what they entail. Calendars and schedules should be used to help us plan our time effectively, not to enslave us.

The effect of procrastination is restricted when you have a deadline. You know you can put things off until tomorrow, and then rush to complete the work just the night before the deadline. We have all made this same mistake which is not so bad because it works out in the end, sort of. There is another problem, though. We stop procrastinating when we are met with a deadline. What if the deadline is not there? There is one for the assignment or project. But what of other things such as visiting your family, taking care of your health, exercising, working on your relationship, or working on yourself? They don't have deadlines, do they? This is where procrastinating becomes very deadly. The deadline is not there, so we do not feel as compelled to do something, but then we would regret not doing it until it is too late.

Regardless of which category you fall into, know that time is limited. We tend to think that we have plenty of time. We actually don't. Let us put this into perspective.

In the United States, the average lifespan of a person is 27,375 days. If you are 25, then you have 18,250 days to live. If you are 50, you have roughly 9,125 days, and if you are 65, 3,650 days. As you can see, we do not have much time in our lives. To make matters worse, suppose that you sleep for eight hours a day. That is already a third of your time spent just on sleeping alone. Do you have an 8-hour job? That's another third. We have roughly 34% of our time to waste on other things such as watching TV, listening to music, and basically procrastinating. Are you willing to risk what little time you have on these things? Make every second count.

## On Sorting Out Your Priorities

We all strive to do more in our lives. We get out there, chase after our goals and dreams, and make connections. Only when we have those can we make our mark in this world. However, you will tire eventually. After all, we can do anything but not everything. We can only do so much. There are only 24 hours a day, so there is only so much we can do no matter how productive or effective we are.

To make matters worse, our decision-making is lacking compared to the abundance of information and choices available. We pursue all the opportunities we see without stopping to think carefully. We decide not to decide carefully. There is nothing wrong pursuing opportunities, but you will reach a saturation point eventually. You will reach a point where there are so many responsibilities you need to fulfill that you cannot commit to a better role or fulfill your obligations. By then, you will be burned out and it's too late.

It appears that there is a better way to go about managing your time. We all know this, and yet we keep wasting our time on trivial matters. Why is that?

**Hell Yeah Or No**

Derek Sivers wasn't planning on establishing a large business when he started CD Baby. He just wanted to sell his CDs online, but he became a successful independent musician. When he could not find anyone to help him, he went out on his own and built an online store from scratch. It worked out for him very well because he never stopped chasing down opportunities and putting himself out there.

However, somewhere down the road, he, Derek realized something.

He realized that he was not always happy about networking or attending conferences. These things led him to develop a habit of agreeing to do more and more out of obligation, which took away his valuable time and money. He had set himself up to make default choices that were not always the best for him.

From that point on, he created a new philosophy to guide his decisions, especially when he was about to make a commitment. This was to prevent him from overcommitting. It the philosophy goes like this:

"If you're not saying "HELL YEAH!" about something, say "no." When you say no to most things, you leave room in your life to really throw yourself completely into that rare thing that makes you say "HELL YEAH!"

This may not make sense to those who do not make the most of their time, though. If you fall into this category, then by all means, put yourself out there and pursue opportunities. However, this is often not the case for many of us. We have opportunities that we are capitalizing on, but we always want more.

Derek said in his book "Anything You Want," that we only have a limited amount of time every day. So, we all should strive to make the most out of it while we still have enough room to capitalize on better opportunities. Only work on the things that are meaningful and that you care about. Saying yes to less is the way to go.

**The 90% Rule**

Time is the most valuable commodity and trade-offs are often needed when you are at full capacity. Your entire life boils down to a series of transactions – time and money for something else. Everything you do has an opportunity cost and it may be more costly than not doing anything.

Therefore, we all need an essentialist approach to life. It is prioritizing your tasks based on the time you have, and knowing that we need to practice self-selection to really thrive.

Greg McKeown also advocates for this in the book called "Essentialism." He said that only when you allow yourself to stop trying to do everything, to stop saying yes, can you make the highest contribution to things that really matter.

McKeown gives his 90 percent rule: Every opportunity should be scrutinized under extreme criteria. We should pursue opportunities that are rated at 9 on the scale from 1 to 10. No matter how good the 7s and 8s are, we should pass that up unless we are absolutely sure that we have more time to spare for the 9s and 10s. Remember those good opportunities are different from the right ones.

McKeown knows that there are many trivial opportunities that may be good, but not as important or meaningful. There are only a few that mean the most to him. Again, we only have so much time, so we should pursue opportunities that help us to reach where we want to go. Therefore, it is essential that you only commit to the vital few commitments that are important to you.

**Fear of Missing Out**

Of course, we cannot accurately assess whether the opportunity is just good, or important to us.

When we talk about living a better life, we tend to talk about adding more things rather than simplifying and removing things from our lives. As we become more and more interconnected thanks to the Internet, we are more easily influenced by each other as well. If a friend of yours does something, you feel compelled to join in because we would feel excluded and anxious otherwise.

There is actually a name for this: FOMO (fear of missing out), aka peer pressure.

This fear is everywhere, and you probably have experienced it yourself in middle or high school. It is the fear that you may be missing out on an opportunity or the fear that you did not meet someone you should or the fear that you are lagging behind. We struggle with FOMO throughout our lives, no matter how old we are. FOMO is also one of the reasons why we overcommit.

Here, McKeown proposed that we should adopt the joy of missing out (JOMO). The problem with FOMO is that we think we may be missing out on something important. We just need to turn that thinking around and realize that the opportunities we are often given are not the ones that we actually need. Relish the fact that you are missing out on non-essential opportunities and place value on saying no. Know that passing on opportunities may create an opportunity as well.

We have given too much value on getting more and more when we should have been careful in what we invest in, and be happy with what little we have that actually matters.

## A Question of Priorities

We tend not to have our lives straight. We often fail to prioritize the things we should really do, and if we don't somebody else will.

We prioritize different things based on our needs. We have a list of things that we consider to be priorities, and the list can be short or long. But when we prioritize everything, we prioritize nothing. As McKeown explained in Essentialism:

> "The word priority came into the English language in the 1400s. It was singular. It meant the very first or prior thing. It stayed singular for the next five hundred years. Only in the 1900s did we pluralize the term and start talking about priorities. Illogically, we reasoned that by changing the word, we could bend reality. Somehow we would now be able to have multiple "first" things."

While having multiple priorities gives us some comfort because it shows that we have some level of ambition and makes us feel that we are making progress, in reality, it only distracts us from what is really important. When you start to internalize this truth, it gets easier for you to simplify your life and start doing less. Every time you refuse to get involved in doing something trivial, you create an opportunity for better things to come along or it gives you time to focus on working toward your goal. Trivial things are not worth our attention, so we should embrace JOMO.

# On Trusting the Process

With a whopping 6 National Championships under his belt, Nick Saban, a football coach from the University of Alabama, is one of the best college football coaches the world has ever seen.

Although his names are often associated with victory, Saban does not care too much about the end result. The final scoreboard does not mean much to him. Instead, he wants his assistant coaches and players to just focus on the process. This is what he said:

"Don't think about winning the SEC Championship. Don't think about the national championship. Think about what you need to do in this drill, on this play, at this moment. That's the process: Let's think about what we can do today, the task at hand."

This is a different perspective and it is quite refreshing. Some coaches may try to hype up their players because this is a winner-takes-all situation. You may think that it is a good idea to let your own players know what is at stake because you either win or you lose. There are no moral victories or consolidating prizes here. If you don't win, you leave empty-handed. But why does Nick Saban just focus on the process? Let us take a closer look.

### You Can Only Control the Process

Sports are complex. There are many things we need to take into consideration. Many of these variables are not within the control of both the players and coaches. There are so many plays a player can make in a given situation, so many statistics, and so many countermoves that it is literally impossible for each player or coach to know or memorize. To control the entire process is pure madness.

After Nick talked to psychiatry professor Lionel Rosen, he realized that the average play players make lasts only seven seconds. So, he simplified the entire process. If it is impossible to read and execute every play to perfection for the entire match, why not just focus on those seven seconds? Maintaining perfect execution for the entire game is asking for too much, but anyone can execute a play that lasts for seven seconds with perfection. So, just execute the play, rest, and repeat. Then, you will eventually have the game.

Excellence is a step-by-step process. It requires you to excel at the first, second, third thing, and so on. The process is all about staying in the present and going through with the action that you excel in, one after another. You need to focus on executing these actions regardless of the obstacles in your way.

This was exactly what Saban's team did, and they started winning games and championships.

## It's the Inner Scoreboard That Counts

If you have seen his team playing, then the sight of Saban scowling on the sidelines may be pretty common for you even though his team was winning the game by a big margin. If you don't know him, you may think that he is on the losing team. Why is that? As he told ESPN:

"I know I get criticized for that. Everybody says, 'He just won 31–3. What's he complaining about?' But it goes back to the inner scoreboard versus the outer scoreboard. Which one is more important? If you're going to accomplish your goals, it's always the inner scoreboard."

He was upset about the little things. It could be because someone didn't follow the play that he planned, or maybe someone was not in their position. It may be the fact that everyone did not perform at their very best.

You may think that these errors should be overlooked when the team is winning, but not for Nick Saban. Even during practice, he wants his players to achieve peak performance.

Saban knew if a player had completed his workouts. He made sure that every single drill was done perfectly. He checked whether his players had followed the dress code. He even had a rule that players could not droop their shoulders even though this was a normal posture after practice when they were exhausted. All of these rules point to one question "How good do you want to be?"

We mentioned earlier how little things can snowball into big things. The first place winner does not win by a mile. More often than not, the second place is only behind by a nose. So, every little thing counts. If you do more things correctly than your opponents, you will eventually come out on top. Saban knew that very well and made sure that every little thing went right. If his team did not execute those small actions properly, they did not deserve to win.

To Saban, the outer scoreboard does not matter. It does not always show what you have done right. Instead, we should all have our own inner scoreboard to keep track of our progress.

## Keep Moving Forward

Having a goal alone is not enough. It tells you what you should strive forward, but it does not tell you what you need to do to reach that end. This is why you need a couple of goals with an action plan – the process. It gives you a checklist of items to tick off. That way, you know what the next step is to reach your goal. You know where you are and you are accountable for your actions.

Goals are also relatively short-term. They give you a boost in confidence when you overcome them, but they may cause you to become complacent. If you fail, it is difficult for you to recover and get yourself sorted again.

On the other hand, if you follow a process, you know that there is something you should do. If you miss a workout or make a mistake, you can always aim to get it next time around. The process gears you up toward long-term thinking because it is all about commitment and following a plan over a long time.

Entrepreneur Gary Vaynerchuk often talks about "macro patience, micro speed." This is the spirit behind the process. Nowadays, many of us develop instant gratification thanks to the internet. We become impatient and worry about what will happen in a few years. Yet, we spend our days making poor decisions and wasting our time.

To get our lives sorted, we need to have a process we can follow. DO not become so enamored with your goals that you forget what you should be doing right now. Have a set goal and design a process to achieve it, and then commit to the process. Simply put, do your job.

## On Dealing with Anger

How do we become angry? This is a predictable emotion for the Stoics, not unforeseeable mishaps. It is not an automatic response that we cannot control, either. So when someone does something offensive, when they do something harmful, offensive, threatening, or wrong, we will react with anger. We follow a process in which we get angry. Understanding this process, and how it works, can lead us to manage our anger over time.

We can examine our thought process by understanding anger as an emotional and bodily response, not just raw affectivity. There is an underlying thought-process driving it. So, we at least know that this is something we can control. Epictetus said that our work, our choices, desires, denials, assents, judgments, and assumptions are the things that are in our control.

As a rule of thumb, when we get angry, we are wrong in our evaluation of what is happening and in our reasoning about the matter in relation to other things. Simply put, anger results from what we think is good and bad, how we order and value things, and what we desire and are averse to.

If we want to manage and master our own emotions, we need to understand them first. This entails examining what we value, what we think is good and bad, and our own desires. If we can be honest with ourselves, we can assess the situation better and perhaps identify the things that are outside our scope of power. These things are not good or bad per se, but we still treat them as such because we feel they are good or bad. As we have covered in a previous chapter, we should not allow external events to influence our emotions. In this case, we would be wrong in our assumption if we determine something to be good or bad if it is outside our area of control.

By doing so, we make ourselves vulnerable to the world, especially to those who are not rational. As Epictetus pointed out, the only thing you can predict about them is to study their thought process – to learn what seems rational to them but isn't in reality.

But let us not talk about those people, as we cannot control their behavior. What we want to work on is ourselves. How exactly do we get our assumptions wrong in the first place? Of course, it depends on the person in certain situations. Among all of the unique events, there are certain commonalities we can pick out. One of which is the assumption that whatever happened or has been done to us, should not or should never have occurred.

What causes this "should not" assumption in our thought process? At the bottom, it comes from our desire for things to go our way, the things that are outside our control. We want to cling onto things that may possibly be ours, but don't necessarily have to be. We also want others to treat us in certain ways and not in others because we see their actions and words as indicators of what they think and feel about us. Basically, we want a perfect world in which people and events go our way. Of course, this is not the case, so we feel wronged, become angry, and want revenge.

## Addressing Anger As It Arises

It is worth developing an understanding of our irrationality, its negative consequences or how it is counterproductive to our lives. For some, these insights might even be needed if they want to control or address their anger. Of course, just by getting a firm grasp of our weak points in our character and our own thought process does not change much.

We can analyze, scrutinize, or reflect on ourselves without really addressing the problem. In fact, we may become complacent and replace practical effort with contemplative work. Epictetus also talked about this, criticizing those who confused studying and putting what they've learned into practice. It is possible to go one step further but it still does not resolve problems. We can make all sorts of plans and resolutions, even complex ones, and still not get very far with keeping our anger under control.

Therefore, the best way to go forward is by doing something about it. When we realize that our emotional response, anger, is detrimental to our peace of mind, we can begin to put in conscious efforts into controlling our emotions. If you recognize that your anger is something that is bad for you and really want to do something about it, then you need to choose some of the most effective means to that end. How effective they are is determined by how much effort you put into practicing them.

We need to remind ourselves that what is at stake is the motivation we all need to deal with our own anger, which is far from a walk in the park. Controlling our own emotions means opposing a part of ourselves that is pressing upon us, messing us up through the process, and dominating how we should think and feel. If we wish to go on the Stoic path, we need to resist that part of ourselves. So, what can we do to manage our anger? In the book titled "Discourse," Epictetus offered us several concrete actions we can act upon.

### Understand Why

As we mentioned earlier, people have a reason for their behavior. The reason is quite understandable as well if we put ourselves in their shoes. While those who anger us often do not think rationally, what they do does seem rational to them. We have different thought processes, emotional responses, desires, etc. so what they think is logical to them may not be so logical to us. If we can understand what they do as partly rational and partly irrational, it will make sense that they act this way. We will then be less bothered by it.

## Distancing From the Appearances

Every day, we are faced with all sorts of appearances that tell us how they should be interpreted and played into our network of desires and aversions, assumptions and opinions. We do not have to assent to them automatically, especially to those that upset us. These appearances have to do with harm or insult to ourselves when others want to harm or insult us. So, just see them as events that happen and remain neutral about the whole thing. Again, it is not the outside mishap that upsets us, it is how we perceive and react to it.

## Remind Ourselves of Our Humanity

When we fail morally, we resemble a class of animals metaphorically. Anger is associated with beasts of prey, engaging in activities appropriate for their class as animals, but not for us as humans. This is a classic anger management technique. When we liken our reactions to animals, we bring ourselves before our eyes and are, therefore, able to determine what we'd look like when we become angry. At the same time, we can remind ourselves that we are not animals. We are humans who are capable of choosing how we can respond and how we can approach problems rationally.

## Removing Ourselves from Competition

If we take what other people see as goods, which are often external (outside our control), to be meaningful and genuine goods, we will be dragged into conflict with others over those goods. We may even experience conflict with ourselves as well because what we believe to be good may not be good to others. When we try to pursue the goods from both perspectives, it can create a rift in ourselves. So, to combat this, we need to remind ourselves that what we are pursuing are external things that do not necessarily make us happy. You do not need to struggle against other people to get it.

## Fulfilling Your Roles towards Others

When we get angry at someone and act upon that anger towards them, we normally transgress the role and its associated duties in relation to those people. We have a choice here. We can maintain or restore that role in ourselves. Your roles can be a friend, a citizen, a family member, a neighbor, etc. Restore that role, or give in to anger. It can be hard to remain friends with someone that you are angry with. We can also place our anger on the fact that they failed to fulfill their own roles towards us. This means that your anger stems from their failures, not yours so you can calm yourself down because this is not something you should waste time and energy on. Their failure is outside your control, after all.

# Chapter 8: On the Art of Mental Toughness

What do you think determines how far you will go in life? Is it wealth, health, fame, or something else?

This tough question has been asked and answered for ages. Back in the '60s, Stanford professor Walter Mischel conducted the Marshmallow experiment. Here, children had to choose whether they could get one marshmallow right away, or wait a little longer to get two.

Those who decided to wait for two reported doing better in life in general, even forty years later. This ability to delay gratification is also related to higher SAT scores, lower levels of substance abuse, lower likelihood of obesity, and many other indicators of success.

After that, Angela Duckworth documented the results of her research in her book titled "Grit" the following:

- West Point cadets who got the highest score on the Grit Test were 60% more likely to succeed than their peers.
- Ivy League undergraduate students who were mentally tough also had a higher GPA than their peers even though they had lower SAT scores and weren't perceived as "smart."
- When comparing two people who are the same age and have different levels of education, the level of mental toughness (but not intelligence) more accurately determines who will be better educated.

From what we can tell from these studies, we can say with certainty that characteristics such as grit, perseverance, and self-control are key to success. We can put them under the mental toughness umbrella. Therefore, if you want to go far in life, mental toughness is key. So, how do we go about reinforcing our minds?

## Deconstruct Things

To start with, you need to remain steadfast, unintimidated by the challenges ahead of you. In many cases, we become paralyzed by the sheer size of the obstacle that we end up throwing our hands up and resigning instead of working to overcome it and reach our goal.

So, when you are faced with an obstacle, the first step would be to deconstruct it into bite-sized chunks. You have to break it down into small actionable steps to allow you to tackle the problem. When you break things down into bite-sized chunks, you can create a process that you can follow to tackle the problem. This allows you to track your own progress, giving you a sense of control, and eventually allowing you to overcome the problem.

When you allow yourself to remain steadfast in the face of an insurmountable obstacle, you create an opportunity for yourself to remain calm and rational so you can assess the situation properly. This is how successful people manage to maintain their peak performance even in stressful situations. They do not capitulate when they have to climb a mountain because they break down the mountain into individual steps. Anyone can take a step forward. These people know how far and how fast they need to climb.

Going up just a meter allows you to chalk up a small victory, giving you the mental strength to go onward. Marathoners have the same mindset. They do not think that they need to run 26 miles. They just focus on their pace and the next landmark. That gives them a more realistic goal to pursue.

## Reframe Negative Events

"Men are disturbed not by things, but the view they take of them." – Epictetus

If you didn't know already, life is unfair and it will beat you senseless at certain points. This is something that you cannot change. So, the Stoic approach here is to not worry about what comes your way, but rather prepare yourself mentally on how you want to react to it.

Mentally resilient individuals do not view failure as a knockout punch. Instead, they brush it off as a bruise and continue on ahead. They know that their plan is not without flaws and they expect failures. This is just as good a feedback as success. Failure is not a condemnation of their abilities. It is nothing personal.

In the book "The Startup of You," Reid Hoffman urges people to remain in the state of "permanent beta." Similar to products released for testing, flaws are to be expected. So are you. You cannot expect yourself to be the perfect human being. The path to perfection is long, with success and failures. By putting yourself in this state, you allow yourself space to improve as you expect to encounter a lot of obstacles. You see each failure as feedback from which you can improve quickly. So, you are a work-in-progress.

As Thomas Edison once said, "I have not failed. I've just found 10,000 ways that won't work." This is the view you need to adopt if you want to go far in life. The more you try, the more mistakes you will make. But that is not necessarily a bad thing. Trying and failing is always better than not trying at all. In order to grow and develop, you need to step out of your comfort zone, which involves risks. Mentally strong individuals do not allow themselves to be weighed down by negative mishaps. So shouldn't you. This is not about optimism, either. This wishful thinking alone gives you mental strength, but it will not get you very far.

## Acknowledge Your Challenges

Admiral Jim Stockdale was taken prisoner during the Vietnam War. The Viet Cong did not follow any humanitarian treaties, so they treated prisoners as they pleased. You can imagine what they did to him. He was tortured over twenty times during his eight-year imprisonment from 1965 to 1973. He miraculously survived the war even though he had no prisoner's rights, no set release date, and no certainty on whether he would even survive to see his beloved family again.

Still, even when the situation looked grim for him, Stockdale never lost hope. He said that he never doubted the fact that he would get out, and that he would prevail in the end and then turn this horrible experience into the defining experience in his life. This was something he would not trade in retrospect.

So, was this just sheer optimism? This is known as the Stockdale paradox, as he mentioned that it was always the most optimistic prison mates that failed to survive the imprisonment. He said:

"They were the ones who said, 'We're going to be out by Christmas.' And Christmas would come, and Christmas would go. Then they'd say, 'We're going to be out by Easter.' And Easter would come, and Easter would go. And then Thanksgiving, and then it would be Christmas again. And they died of a broken heart."

This is the Stockdale paradox. Jim Collins noted in his book "Good to Great," self-deception can help you overcome short-term discomfort or embarrassment. However, it is unhealthy in the long run as it will come back to haunt you.

Therefore, pure optimism is not the way to go. You must balance optimism with realism. You need to acknowledge that the difficulties are real and you need to be willing to pay the price. Most of the time, people lose hope because of their unrealistic assessment and expectation of the situation. They become overwhelmed when reality sets in, and they are faced with a sense of helplessness.

"You must never confuse faith that you will prevail in the end — which you cannot afford to lose — with the discipline to confront the most brutal facts of your current reality, whatever they might be." – Jim Stockdale

## Find Your Purpose

Angela Duckworth said that grit is the perseverance and passion to achieve a long-term goal. She interviewed those with exceptional grit and noted that every one of them pursues something that has a purpose.

So, what is purpose?

There is no general definition, so it is up to you to define. What we all agree on is that purpose gives you a powerful motivation to succeed even if the odds are stacked against you. It keeps you going even when you are faced with agonizing pain. You keep pushing through the pain because you know the pain of discipline hurts less than the pain of regret. This is the power of purpose.

Purpose does not need to be a big or abstract concept, either. You just need to look to something or someone that you care about. You will find your purpose there.

A soldier may fight hard for his comrade beside him, or for his country. A mother may wake up in the middle of the night because her infant cries, and she may cajole him back to sleep. Activists, though their actions seem insignificant and may not influence major political decisions, still gather around and get as much support as possible to voice their demands. People are willing to work tirelessly if they work toward something that they believe in, no matter the obstacle.

"He who has a why to live can bear almost any how." – Friedrich Nietzsche

Mentally resilient individuals can bear all their trails and errors in their attempt to achieve their goal because they have an intrinsic driving force. As a result, they can remain steadfast and push forward even through difficult times.

## Recharge and Recover

While mental resilience often gives you an image of a person weathering all hardships, no one can do it infinitely. A large portion of mental toughness is recovery. After all, we have biological limits to what we can take.

Our mind becomes ineffective if it is put through too much stress over a period of time. Just like your muscles, your willpower can get burnt out eventually. Researchers call this the decision fatigue because every single decision we make reduces our willpower. Here, every little decision counts.

Barack Obama and Mark Zuckerberg are known for the fact that they wear the same clothing every day. They do this to conserve their willpower. As a result, they can make better decisions when a lot of things are at stake.

Shawn Achor and Michelle Gielan argued in their Harvard Business Review that it is all about how you recover, and not how you endure a hard time. They wrote that the key to resilience is doing your best, then pausing, recovering, and then trying again. We need to rest now and again in order to achieve peak performance.

Do not let work drain you of your willpower even when you are not there. Give yourself time to rest, recharge, and be immersed in the moment. This is why mindful practices are critical for mental tranquility. Whenever you can, get off your social media accounts and emails. These things force you to kind of keep chugging on, which is not going to help you in the long run. When you do this, you do not allow your brain to recover and prepare for the next stressful event because you plug into another source of mental stimulus. So, get enough rest and recover properly.

Mentally resilient individuals ensure that they get enough rest. So, they have enough mental strength to last through even the toughest times. You should strive to do the same if you want to really reinforce your mind.

## Flex the Muscle

Mental toughness is a skill, meaning that you can develop it through constant practice and conscious effort. As with anything involving personal growth, you will need to step outside your comfort zone and learn to be comfortable being uncomfortable. This is true when you need to increase your mental resilience since you can only tap into this strength when you are faced with a difficult challenge. Therefore, mental toughness is one of the most critical characteristics to develop.

Navy SEALs adopt the 40% rule that they live by. Basically, when your mind tells you that you are done, you are only 40% done. This is why almost all runners that participate in a marathon finish when most ordinary people stop at mile 16.

This means going the extra mile and pushing yourself through the brutal conditions. Keep taking that one extra step, even if you are out of breath. Are your arms burning? Give yourself one more rep. As Winston Churchill says, "if you're going through hell, keep going."

Many people would've given up when they grew tired, but not you. This gives you an edge in life as well because it shows others that you can succeed where others tend to fail.

## Stay Resilient

Life is unfair. It will beat you down to your knees and make sure you stay down if you allow it. To go far ahead in life, you need to strengthen your mind to overcome even the most difficult obstacles and recover from the most painful failures. When you do, you will realize that there is no river too wide or mountain too tall. You can overcome anything.

# Chapter 9: Other Practical Tips and Practices

Other than all the other practical advice we have covered, these are some of the tips that do not quite fit in with others.

## Add a Reserve Clause – If Nothing Prevents You

"I will sail across the ocean if nothing prevents me." – Seneca

We have mentioned time and again that it is vital that you know that everything is not under your control. You can only do a few things. The Stoics know that well, so they say that they will try to do something, "as long as nothing prevents" them. This reserve clause helps tone down our expectations somewhat and reminds us that there is always uncertainty in the things that we do.

We do not know what tomorrow will bring. As they used to say, come what may. Here, the Stoics take it a step further. They put all of their efforts into doing something, but they know very well that the ultimate outcome is beyond their direct control. They accept this fact, so whatever the result is, they know that they are not to blame. They eliminated the fact that their laziness or carelessness led them to their failure. They did their best, so they have no reason to blame themselves if the outcome does not turn out to be the way they expected.

This exercise works like this: When you are going to do something, add a reserve clause like "God willing," or "if nothing prevents me."

- I'll finish this project today if nothing prevents me.
- See you tomorrow, if nothing happens.
- I'll give voluntary discomfort and go a week without the internet if nothing prevents me.

## Love Your Fate

"Fate leads the willing, and drags along the reluctant." – Seneca

While we are on the topic of control, let us talk about fate. People say that we are masters of our own fate, but we do not have as much control over it as we think. The Stoics advised us not to wish for the reality to be any different. Instead, we should all accept and love it as it is. They say that fate is like a moving cart, and we are the dog that is leashed to it.

A foolish man would tug and bite at the leash, fighting the cart as it moves along. In the end, they would still be dragged with the cart anyway, no matter how hard he struggles. On the other hand, a wise man would be in the same situation, but he would run alongside the cart, keeping pace with it.

You cannot change what happens in life, so the best thing to do is to just accept it rather than fight every insignificant thing that happens. We're the dog that is leashed to the cart and the only thing we can control is how close we want to be to that cart. Even that is limited. So, instead of being dragged along, we might as well enjoy the journey.

To resent what happens means that you assume that you have a say in the matter. We do not.

So, whenever something happens to you, ask yourself whether you can do something about it. If yes, then do something about it. If not, then it's not under your control. Its fate, so accept it as it is. There is no point in fighting it because it will only make you look bitter and miserable. You need to adopt these three principles:

- Nonattachment: Everything has its end, so do not get too attached to what you like.
- Nonjudgment: Do not judge the event. It changes nothing. Accept them as they are.
- Nonresistance: Do not wish the reality to be any different.

## Forgive the Wrongs of Others

"When a man asserts, then, to what is false, know that he had no wish to assent to the false: 'for no soul is robbed of the truth with its own consent,' as Plato says, but the false seemed to him true." – Epictetus

The Stoics believe that everyone tries to do the right thing, even though it is actually not the case. Most of the time, we do not commit a wrong on purpose. Therefore, we should treat those who misbehave with pity rather than blame.

After all, is it fair for us to be angry at someone when we know that that person doesn't know any better? That is why we need to be tolerant and kind instead. We should learn to forgive others. As Jesus said, "Father, forgive them, for they don't know what they are doing."

So, before you get angry with someone, stop and tell yourself that the person does not know any better. In doing so, you can calm yourself and be kind and forgiving.

- Do not seek revenge when someone wrongs you: It comes from weakness, so be strong and choose to be tolerant and kind instead.
- Pity instead of blame: They are merely blinded by their own mind.
- If someone is being impolite to you, try to see it as a way to train your mind. We all learn and try to become better people. So, this is your chance to train your mental resilience. Shake it off and move on.

## Buy Tranquility

"Starting with things of little value – a bit of spilled oil, a little stolen wine – repeat to yourself: 'For such a small price I buy tranquility and peace of mind." – Epictetus

This is what all Stoics strive towards. One of the things they excel at is staying calm even in the face of adversity. No matter what comes his way, he remains calm and collected.

"I buy tranquility instead," is a sentence we should tell ourselves. It can save us a lot of mental energy. When something happens that you do not like and that arouses your anger and excitement, tell yourself, "I buy tranquility instead." Then, move on calmly, with a smile.

Try to incorporate this quote into your life. It will be worth it. Of course, it requires you to be aware of your own emotions and step in between the stimulus and your response. If you can stop the former from reaching the latter, you can benefit from this quote.

So, try to be aware of your life. When something happens that makes you feel discontent or angry, tell yourself, "I buy tranquility instead."

- When you spill some coffee on your clothes – buy tranquility instead.
- When your roommate doesn't do the dishes – buy tranquility instead.
- When the person driving in front of you is going too slow – buy tranquility instead.

## 16 Lessons for Living

In the thirty-third part of Epictetus' Handbook, you will find plenty of good advice for living a meaningful, happy life. It is the longest part of the Encheiridion and gives an insight into the best practices in a wide range of areas, especially in a social situation. It is a good idea to adopt these lessons, but there is no need to follow every single one of them. It is okay if you disagree with some of them, as these lessons may not be applicable in your situation. These 16 lessons are:

1. Create a type of character and model for yourself that you will follow no matter what.
2. Keep quiet and speak what is required, but sparingly. Only when communication is needed, speak. Again, do not speak about trivialities such as the everyday subjects and especially about other people to blame them, praise them, or compare them.
3. When you can, speak up to lead the conversation to what is proper. If you find yourself in a company that thinks differently, then remain silent.
4. Do not laugh at many things, or much, or without restraint.
5. Never make promises if you can. If not, refuse as far as you can.
6. Do not go to parties hosted by an outsider or a layman. However, if you find yourself in such a situation, focus your attention and do not get in the way of a layman. If your companion is stained with wine, anyone who rubs against him will be just as dirty if that person happens to be clean himself.
7. For your body, you only need the bare necessities such as food, drink, clothes, and shelter. Reject anything that is for show or for pure luxury.
8. If possible, keep clear of sex before marriage. If you do engage in it, keep it appropriate. Do not provoke or shun anyone that engages in it. Also, do not bring forward the fact that you do not engage in it yourself.
9. If someone tells you that someone else talked about you behind your back, do not defend yourself against the claim. Instead, say that the person must not be aware of your other faults, else he would not have mentioned only what he said.
10. You do not need to go to an award show often. If you go, do not show that you support anyone else except yourself. Only yearn for what happens as it happens, and only that the winner takes the prize. This way, you will not be let down. Stop yourself from shouting or cheering for someone, or getting too excited. After everything ends, do not speak of what happened if it does not lead to your own improvement. Otherwise, others would think that you were captivated by the show.
11. Do not go into someone's presentation so casually or at random. If you must, preserve your dignity and composure as you go, while trying your best to not be a nuisance.

12. When you are about to meet someone, especially a high-ranking individual, think of what Zeno or Socrates would do in your situation. You can never go wrong by behaving like them in the encounter.
13. When you are about to visit someone with great power, imagine that you will not find him at home, or that you will be shut out, or that his doors will be slammed in your face, or that he will not notice you. With all of this in mind, if you still think that you should visit that person, then think about what may happen during the visit and never tell yourself that it's not worth that much. Doing so is like a fool and someone who is affected by external things.
14. When you are with other people, refrain from describing your own achievements and adventures excessively or frequently. It may be pleasant for you to recall your epic tales, but it is not the case for others who have to listen to you.
15. At the same time, try not to evoke laughter. This can lead quickly to vulgarity and can cause those around you to lose respect for you.
16. It is risky to use obscene language as well. Whenever someone else uses it, rebuke that person. If that's not possible, try to show your disapproval about their use of language by keeping quiet, blushing, or looking visibly stern.

# Chapter 10: Conclusion

That is all you need to know to start your journey down a path of virtue toward mental tranquility and meaningful life. Ancient philosophers have given us much to learn about the idea of Stoicism, and it is highly recommended that you check out their works.

To wrap everything up, there is one more tip worth mentioning. Do not be too harsh on yourself. Living a Stoic life can be difficult for many people as it requires you to detach from material possessions. Try your best to lead a good life and act appropriately in social situations. Follow what the Stoics said. You can never go wrong. At the same time, do not beat yourself up too harshly if you fail to follow one of their teachings. We are all humans, after all. What matters is that you keep up the effort in improving yourself.

With that in mind, good luck with your journey.

www.ingramcontent.com/pod-product-compliance
Lightning Source LLC
Chambersburg PA
CBHW081154070526
44583CB00021B/2827